Sound Partners

Patricia Vadasy

Susan Wayne

Rollanda O'Connor

Joseph Jenkins

Kathleen Pool

Mary Firebaugh

Julia Peyton

A Tutoring

Program in

Phonics-Based

Early Reading

TUTOR HANDBOOK

Sopris West®
EDUCATIONAL SERVICES
A Cambium Learning® Company
BOSTON, MA · LONGMONT, CO

D1557782

Printed in the United States of America
Published and Distributed by

Sopris West®
EDUCATIONAL SERVICES

A Cambium Learning® Company

17855 Dallas Parkway, Suite 400 ▸ Dallas, TX 75287
800 547-6747 ▸ www.voyagersopris.com

Acknowledgments

We accumulated an extended debt of gratitude over the decade that we designed, field-tested, revised, and evaluated *Sound Partners*. Many individuals and agencies made important contributions to these lessons. The development and research on *Sound Partners* was supported by a series of grants from the U.S. Department of Education, Office of Special Education Programs, and a grant from the Paul Allen Charitable Foundation. Without the support provided by these grants, the development of *Sound Partners* would not have been possible.

Sound Partners is one translation of the rich research base on beginning reading development and instruction. We are indebted to the researchers who built the strong foundation on which applied researchers like ourselves can confidently develop effective applications for practitioners.

Staff and consultants who have contributed to the research and development of the program include: Robert Abbott, Roslyn Adams, Tove Andvik, Lynn Barnicle, Pieter Drummond, Carolyn Hahne, Sally Hurley, Norris Phillips, Scott Stage, Kris Van Valkenberg, and Lynn Youngblood. Many tutors provided immensely valuable feedback and suggestions, including Beverly DeCook, Rayma Haas, Robin Horton, Jeri Lee, Sandy Humphries, Kit Owen, Katia Roberts, Linda Romanelli, Helene Romero, and Janet Stoeve. Elizabeth Sanders oversaw data management and analysis in our series of evaluations of *Sound Partners*.

The principals and staff (including each building's school secretary who assisted in scheduling, testing, and obtaining parent consents) of our Seattle School District sites made it possible for us to conduct our research and intervention in their buildings. Special thanks go to Cathy Profilet-Shibayama, principal, Viewlands Elementary; Val Wells, Powerful Schools Tutor Coordinator; Greg Tuke, Powerful Schools Executive Director; Susan McCloskey, principal, B.F. Day Elementary; Eric Nelson, principal, Sanislo Elementary; Margo Siegenthaler, Tutor Coordinator, B.F. Day Elementary; and Nancy Chin, principal, Laurelhurst Elementary. We also thank the many teachers in our sites who allowed us to work with the students in their classrooms.

We wish to express our gratitude to Christine Cox, Mary Gallien, Karla Haden, and Kathryn Compton for the typing, design, and preparation of many experimental versions of the lessons.

Finally, we thank all the students and families who have participated in our research on *Sound Partners*.

Contents

Introduction

Before young children begin to read books, they develop an understanding of the parts of words—the individual sounds or phonemes. Children learn that words are made up of sounds that can be put together in different ways, and that these sounds correspond to the letters in the alphabet. Many researchers have studied how these discrete skills—taking words apart into their individual sounds, blending sounds to make words, spelling words, rhyming, recognizing letter patterns—contribute to reading. Very young children learn these skills by being read to, looking at books with parents, following along with the words, and playing with words that rhyme or start with the same sound.

Phonological awareness is the understanding that words are made up of sounds, or phonemes, that can be manipulated. It includes rhyming, counting syllables, and segmenting spoken words into sounds. Before they can read books, children demonstrate levels of phonological awareness. At an early level, children recognize words that rhyme and words that begin with the same letter sounds. At later levels, children can segment a word into its individual phonemes, blend sounds together to make a word, and discriminate the ending and middle sounds of words. The research is clear that children must have phonological processing skills in order to learn to read. These skills enable the child to understand that words are made up of individual sounds, or phonemes, and that these sounds match with letters of the alphabet.

Phonics describes the relationship between letter sounds and written letters. Because English is a complex language, it can be difficult for children to detect the ways the 44 sounds in our language map onto the 26 letters of the alphabet. Research supports the value of direct instruction in phonics and the regularities of the English language and also shows that training in the skills of segmenting, blending, and letter-sound knowledge, along with opportunities to apply these skills in well-chosen storybooks, has a positive effect on reading acquisition.

This research into the value of phonics is so strong and so clear that we set out to make it possible for nonprofessional tutors—paraprofessional staff, as well as caring parents and adults in the school community—to teach these skills to first graders at high risk for reading problems. *Sound Partners* is a way to provide individual instruction in essential early reading skills to those children who need it most. It offers what many reading experts today advocate: a comprehensive and balanced approach to instruction, including instruction in isolated decoding skills as well as meaning-based learning through increasing amounts of storybook reading.

Sound Partners is designed for tutors who are helping first graders or other students who cannot yet decode. Children who experience difficulty with letter-sound and decoding skills need help learning these skills as quickly as possible so that they can keep up with classmates and take advantage of classroom reading instruction. We know that children who are doing poorly in reading at the end of first grade are likely to remain poor readers. It is very difficult to correct reading problems, and children with reading problems are likely to fall farther and farther behind their classmates. Intensive early intervention in the form of individual tutoring is one effective way to prevent reading failure. By tutoring *effectively*, you can reduce the number of students who continue to have reading problems.

Quick Definitions of Key *Sound Partners* Features

▶ **Phonological awareness**—The ability to explicitly reflect on the sound structure of spoken language.

▶ **Segmenting**—Breaking up a word into individual sounds (phonemes).

▶ **Blending**—Running all of the sounds together to make a word.

▶ **Phonics**—Instruction that emphasizes letter-sound relationships.

▶ **Letter-sound correspondence**—Understanding that written letters represent spoken sounds.

Effective *Sound Partners* Tutors:

▶ **Follow the *Sound Partners* lesson format**—They do not improvise or incorrectly deliver instruction.

▶ **Keep a brisk, intensive pace**—Because they are well organized, effective tutors do not have unnecessary pauses between lesson instruction components, and they keep their students engaged.

▶ **Be consistent**—*Sound Partners* is most effective when it is used for tutoring four to five days per week.

▶ **Get to know their students and their students' skills**—They observe student strengths and areas in need of improvement. They add practice on weak areas and move more quickly over material that is easy for the student.

▶ **Use specific praise with their students**—They offer statements such as "I like the way you are using your finger to keep your place. That works very well." This helps students know what they are doing correctly.

Sound Partners Lesson Features

The *Sound Partners* lessons contain common, basic components that change gradually so that lessons proceed in a very predictable fashion for you, the tutor, and your students. The basic components are described in detail in this section.

Early lessons (1–30) cover instruction in most common sounds of individual letters and letter pairs, as well as contain practice in segmenting words into phonemes and a strategy for sounding out unfamiliar words composed of previously taught letter sounds. Spelling practice, word lists, and storybook reading are added throughout the lessons. Irregular or sight words are also taught in the early lessons. In the middle set of lessons (31–60), the phonemic awareness activities are faded out, and more phonics instruction and reading and spelling practice are added, including words with initial/final blends, magic -e- words, and word endings (e.g.,

-**s**, -**ed**, -**ing**, and -**y**). Finally, the later lessons (61–100+) continue to teach letter-sound combinations and introduce strategies for reading longer words. Story reading also takes up a bigger part of lesson time. A detailed Scope and Sequence that describes the lessons and their components can be found before the Appendix section in this handbook.

How to Lay Out Lesson Materials

The lesson pages are designed for the tutor to sit on the right side of the student. This allows you to more easily read the tutor text on the right-hand side of the lesson pages, and the student can more easily read the large print on the left-hand side of each lesson page. *Sound Partners* lessons are laid out in a consistent pattern so that you and your student can sit side by side and easily read and work from your respective parts of the lesson pages.

Boxes Around Letters, Pairs, and Words

A box around a letter, letter pair, or word means that a new sound or word is being introduced, and that the tutor must first model whatever is in the box. You will say, for example: "This is our new letter, m. It makes the sound /m/ like in 'moon.' Now you point to the letter and say the sound." Letter names are underlined, and letter sounds are enclosed by diagonal lines / /.

Tutor Text vs. Student Text

The column of text on the right-hand side of each page includes the tutor directions. This column may contain the directions for a new lesson component, or a reminder for the tutor. This column also contains the tutor's script—what you say to the student to present that particular lesson activity. The tutor script will be enclosed with quotation marks. You do not typically need to prepare any added explanation, unless the student does not understand the directions or needs vocabulary instruction.

Student Reading Procedures

When the student works on each lesson activity, he should read the word lists or letter lists moving from left to right in each row. This will reinforce in the student the left-right orientation of print. The student should always fingerpoint to each item on the lesson page. Fingerpointing increases student accuracy, and it allows you to keep track of which item the student is working on.

Spelling

Whenever the tutor instructions show a pencil icon, direct the student to spell by writing. There are opportunities to practice spelling as a written task in the Say the Sounds, Word Reading, Pair Practice, and Sight Words lesson components. You will dictate several words for the student to write. After the student writes a word, always ask the student to read the word aloud. You can individualize the lessons by giving the student more or less spelling practice, as needed. You will usually begin spelling practice with a newly introduced letter sound or word, one that the student finds difficult, and end with a letter or word that the student can be successful with.

Print Conventions

Letter names are underlined (e.g., <u>a</u>) and letter sounds are enclosed by diagonal lines / / (e.g., the letter sound for the letter <u>a</u> is /a/).

Lesson Coverage

Students will move at different rates through *Sound Partners* lessons. You will begin tutoring your students at Lesson 1 on day one of tutoring, but you may pick up on day two at many different points in the lessons—maybe still on Lesson 1, maybe at the end of Lesson 2. Children participating in our studies completed anywhere from 60 to over 100 lessons by the end of the school year. To ensure that each child makes maximum progress, you must carefully control the pace at which the student works through the lessons. A student who finishes only two lessons in a week may actually make more progress than another who completes four but was merely reviewing material he or she had already mastered.

Finding an appropriate pace for each student is not easy, but it is something that a supervisor can help you with. The program supervisor can show you how to check the student's level of accuracy in each lesson. If a student's responses are correct 95–100% of the time, you may need to move the student forward in the lessons to more challenging material. If the student's performance on a task like sounding out is still only correct 20% of the time when explicit practice on sounding out is about to be phased out of the lessons, then you will need to go back and review at least that section of the lessons until performance improves. Performance on the Mastery Tests (which can be given every 10 lessons) is another way to assess whether a student is placed appropriately and which skills need more practice.

> ### *You may ask . . .*
>
> **If a student is absent, should I skip the lessons he missed, or repeat previous lessons?**
>
> **When a student is absent, you should pick up where you left off at the student's last lesson. Often this is where the student should be. If the student has been having difficulty, or has had a long absence, you may need to go back and repeat lessons, starting with the point where the student is about 90% accurate on lesson content.**

Letter-Sound Instruction

The most common single letter sounds are the short vowels and the consonants. A *continuous* sound is a sound that can be extended for several seconds without distorting the sound, while a *stop* sound is one that can be said for only an instant. Commonly used continuous and stop sounds (and key words for each) are listed on the next page.

The most difficult sounds for students to learn are vowel sounds, as they are very irregular in the English language. Often students will confuse these sounds with one another: /a/ and /e/; /e/ and /i/; and /o/ and /u/.

Sound Partners lessons teach short vowel sounds and use the key words shown below in the Single Letter Sounds section (and on the *Sound Partners* Letter Sounds Cards).

Single Letter Sounds			
Continuous Sounds		**Stop Sounds**	
a	<u>a</u>pple	b	<u>b</u>all
e	<u>E</u>d	c*	<u>c</u>at
f	<u>f</u>ish	d	<u>d</u>og
i	<u>i</u>tch	g*	<u>g</u>irl
l	<u>l</u>ion	h	<u>h</u>at
m	<u>m</u>oon	j	<u>j</u>et
n	<u>n</u>ail	k	<u>k</u>ite
o	<u>o</u>ctopus	p	<u>p</u>ig
r	<u>r</u>at	qu	<u>qu</u>een
s	<u>s</u>un	t	<u>t</u>able
u	<u>u</u>p	x	bo<u>x</u>
v	<u>v</u>et		
w	<u>w</u>indow		
y	<u>y</u>ellow		
z	<u>z</u>ipper		

* These letters also have a soft sound:

c	<u>c</u>ircle	g	<u>g</u>iraffe

Letter Combinations			
Vowel Pairs			
ai	al	ar	ay
r<u>ai</u>n	s<u>al</u>t	c<u>ar</u>	h<u>ay</u>
ea	ee	er	ew
l<u>ea</u>f	tr<u>ee</u>	f<u>er</u>n	scr<u>ew</u>
oa	oi	oo	or
b<u>oa</u>t	<u>oi</u>l	br<u>oo</u>m	f<u>or</u>k
ou	ow	ur	oy
cl<u>ou</u>d	cl<u>ow</u>n	t<u>ur</u>tle	<u>oy</u>ster
Consonant Pairs			
ch	ph	sh	th
<u>ch</u>erry	<u>ph</u>one	<u>sh</u>eep	<u>th</u>umb
	wh	ck	
	<u>wh</u>ale	tru<u>ck</u>	
fl	gr	sl	sk
<u>fl</u>ower	<u>gr</u>ape	<u>sl</u>ide	<u>sk</u>unk
sn	st	sw	tr
<u>sn</u>ail	<u>st</u>op	<u>sw</u>im	<u>tr</u>ain

The following Sample Lessons illustrate the layout and components you will see throughout the *Sound Partners* program.

e E

Ed

Say the Sounds

▶ "Point to each letter. Say the sound."

▶ "Letter e is a vowel, like a, i, o, and u."

m	t	b	u
moon	table	ball	up
e	f	w	d
	fish	window	dog
n	e	f	a
nail			apple
e	j	u	e
	jet		

"Write the letter that makes the _____ sound."

Segmenting

▶ "Break this word into three parts."

pot	hot
cap	wet
Ben	

Sample Lesson 1b

Word Reading

▶ "Sound these out and say them fast."

"What sound does _____ **start** with?"

"What sound does _____ **end** with?"

"What is the **middle/ vowel** sound in _____?"

men	tug	pet
rug	wet	fan
dig	jig	jam
red	Mac	dad
pat	cut	fed

men

"Now you spell _____."

Choose three words for student to spell and read.

Sight Words

come

some

for

can't

his

you

some

come

didn't

is

▶ "This word is _____."

"You read it."

"Point and spell."

"What word?"

▶ *Have student read, point and spell, and then reread each word.*

Dictate three sight words for student to spell and read.

. . . .

Mag can't run. Mag got a cut. Mag didn't run to you or Dad. Mag had a bad leg.

▶ "Read these sentences. Point to each word."

(See the Additional Supplementary Reading Scope and Sequence in the *Tutor Handbook* for additional titles.)

Book Reading

▶ Read *10 Cut Ups.*

Supplementary:
Read *Fun in the Sun.*

Sample Lesson 2a

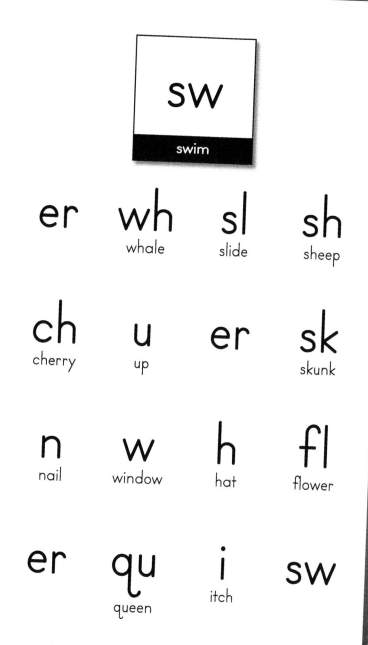

sw
swim

Say the Sounds

▶ "Point to each letter or letter pair. Say the sound."

▶ "Sw makes **two** sounds."

er   wh   sl   sh
      whale   slide   sheep

ch   u   er   sk
cherry   up   skunk

n   w   h   fl
nail   window   hat   flower

er   qu   i   sw
      queen   itch

sl   sh   sw   sk

"Write the letter or letter pair that makes the _____ sound(s)."

Provide the cue word for letter pairs.

Lesson 46 cont'd

Word Reading

▶ "Sound these out and say them fast."

"What sound does _____ **start** with?"

"What sound(s) does _____ **end** with?"

"What is the **middle/ vowel** sound in _____?"

fern

fern	mask	step
slipper	her	whiz
swims	flash	herder
slump	stands	ask
skims	flip	swish

"Now you spell _____."

Choose three words for student to spell and read.

Sample Lesson 2c

Lesson 46 cont'd

vowels: a, e, i, o, u

mate	mat	dime	dim
cam	came	same	Sam
plan	plane	hate	hat

NEW!
Magic -e-

► "Here is the rule: If a word has an e at the end, the middle vowel says its name and the e is quiet. Let's practice this rule."

► *Point to each word and say:*

"Is there an e at the end of this word? Will the middle vowel say its name or its sound?"

"Let's sound out the word."

Word Endings

► *Point to the y:*

"I'm going to say bump with this ending. Bumpy."

"Your turn. Touch the y and say bump with this ending."

► *Repeat with:*

salt	sun
bump	snap

y

► "Now you read these words."

sun	sunny	Tim	Timmy
bug	buggy	flash	flashy
Dan	Danny	Till	Tilly

Reading Long Words

▶ "Long words are made of syllables and are easy to read when we break them up into smaller chunks."

▶ "We can find the syllables by looking for and hearing the vowels."

---

bartering
bar ter ing

▶ "This looks like a difficult word until we break it into three syllables. See, each syllable has a vowel. When we say each syllable, you can feel your mouth open. Each syllable has one beat."

---

un der stand ing

trans port ing

sub tract ing

▶ "First, read these long words already broken into syllables. Then read the word fast."

---

meaningful   smalltime

imperfect   confirming

▶ "Now break these words into syllables, read the syllables, and then read the word."

(See the Additional Supplementary Reading Scope and Sequence in the *Tutor Handbook* for additional titles.)

Book Reading

▶ Read *Samantha.*

Overview of Lesson Components

Each of the *Sound Partners* lessons includes a combination of the following components. Students practice reading (decoding) and spelling (encoding) sounds, words, sentences, and text. Use the Notes section to take down ideas on how to scaffold (e.g., more coaching or added practice) for each component.

Component	Why?	Remember	Note:
Say the Sounds Student practices saying the sound associated with a letter or letter pair and practices writing the letter(s) associated with a sound.	This is an important step toward being able to combine sounds into words.	▶ Model anything in a box, but only sounds, not letter names. ▶ Require fingerpointing. ▶ Use model or key word to correct errors. Have the student repeat correct sound. ▶ Provide extra practice on sounds missed. ▶ Use specific praise.	
Letter Sounds Cards Student practices pairing sounds with key words.	Use as needed to add practice for students not learning sounds at the rate they are introduced in the lessons.	▶ Add practice on 2–3 lines of sounds per day, for 5 minutes at the start of the session. ▶ To help with reading, student points: "a, apple, /a/." ▶ To help with spelling, student points: "apple, /a/, a." ▶ Practice each line both the reading and spelling way.	
Segmenting Student practices listening for the separate sounds in a word and saying them one at a time (in correct sequence).	This builds awareness that words are made up of individual sounds.	▶ This is a listening task. ▶ Model pointing to boxes while saying one sound per box and then saying the whole word. ▶ Correct by modeling and having the student repeat.	

Component	Why?	Remember	Note:
Word Reading Student reads words by saying their sounds and blending them aloud. Student spells words by listening for and writing down the sequence of sounds in the word.	This "sounding out" gives the student a strategy to decode unknown words.	▶ Student should not pause between sounds. ▶ Correct errors by drawing student's attention to the part of the word in error. ▶ Always have the student repeat the word.	
Sight Words Student practices reading words that cannot be sounded out.	The student needs to practice and remember these words by sight.	▶ For correction, model the word and have the student read and spell it aloud (or say the letters)—do not ask the student to sound out sight words.	
Sentence Reading Student reads sentences made up of taught sight and decodable words.	Reading words in sentences helps the student learn that reading has meaning.	▶ Require fingerpointing. ▶ When the student makes an error, require her to reread the entire sentence.	
Magic -e- Student practices reading words using the "magic -e- rule."	This allows the student to read words with long vowel sounds.	▶ Always refer to the rule when correcting.	

Component	Why?	Remember	Note:
Word Endings Student practices reading words with the endings -**s**, -**ed**, -**y**, and -**ing**.	Identifying word endings gives the student another word-attack skill.	▶ Always model the ending as part of a word—never say the ending in isolation (the sound of the ending depends on word context).	
Pair Practice Student practices reading and spelling (writing) words and nonwords with new letter pairs.	This allows student to practice using letter-pair sounds to read and spell.	▶ Correct by directing the student to the letter-pair sound(s).	
Reading Long Words Student practices reading compound and multi-syllable words.	This gives practice in structural analysis—syllable division, inflections, and affixes.	▶ Help the student notice patterns for syllable division. ▶ Correct by having the student read parts of the word and then the whole word.	
Book Reading Student practices reading newly taught sounds and words in a story.	This gives students experience in successful book reading that is matched to their instruction. This practice helps students to become more fluent readers.	▶ Spend more time on book reading as you progress through the lessons. ▶ Use a book-reading method appropriate to the individual student (independent, partner, or echo reading).	

Lesson Mini-Components

Mini-Component	Why?	Remember	Note:
Final <u>m</u> and <u>n</u> Blends Lessons 43–46	Makes explicit the final blends that are nasalized and difficult to hear.	▶ Student reads the word pairs. ▶ Dictate words for student to spell (write).	
Inside-Sound Spelling Lessons 39–42	Makes explicit the initial and final consonant blends by contrasting them to similar words without blends.	▶ Dictate words for student to spell (write).	
Spelling Similar Sounds Lessons 49–51	Makes explicit the **tr** and **ch** sounds that students often confuse due to coarticulation.	▶ Dictate word pairs for student to spell (write).	
Long <u>u</u> Sounds Lessons 53–56	Teaches student that magic -e- can make **u** say either /oo/ or /y-u/.	▶ Student reads, then segments sounds in boxes.	
Useful Word Chunks Lessons 57–59	Teaches student the -**igh** and -**ight** patterns.	▶ Student reads and spells words aloud.	
Double Consonants Lessons 72–74	Provides student with rule for doubling final consonants.	▶ Remind student of rule for consonant doubling. ▶ Dictate words with and without double consonants for student to spell (write).	
Contraction Review Lessons 95 & 99	Provides student with organization of contractions into word families.	▶ Student reads contractions, tells the complete word construction, and tells the missing letters. ▶ Dictate words for student to spell (write).	

Individual Lesson Components

On the following pages we first describe each *Sound Partners* lesson component and then include common questions that you may have about implementing each component.

Say the Sounds (and First Sounds)

In early lessons, individual sounds are taught both in isolation ("*A*. What sound does this letter say?") and in the context of a word ("*Apple*. What's the beginning sound in *apple*?"). The student practices the beginning-sounds activity with difficult letters to facilitate quick retrieval of sounds. Progress in letter-sounds identification is critical to success in the program. Cumulative review of the sounds is built into the lessons. In the second half of the program, the student is introduced to letter combinations, including consonant blends, diphthongs, digraphs, and vowel teams.

It is critical that you, the tutor, model correct letter sounds. An audiotape on letter sounds can be used for training. You will be teaching the short vowel sounds. The vowel sounds will be the most difficult sounds for students to learn and discriminate. Students will confuse /a/ and /e/, /e/ and /i/, and /o/ and /u/. It is very important to model correct vowel sounds.

There are two types of letter sounds: continuous and stop sounds. *Continuous* sounds like /aaa/ and /mmm/ can be stretched out; *stop* sounds like /b/ and /d/ are said quickly. The stop sounds for tutors are: b, d, c, q, t, p, and k. Be careful not to add an "uh" sound after b and d. Stop sounds should be spoken quickly without adding a vowel sound at the end.

If students have difficulty remembering letter sounds, you should use the word cues that pair each letter sound with a word. If the classroom teacher uses a different key word for each letter, use those words. Be consistent and always use the same word (e.g., **/e/** as in **Ed**). The student uses the word to recall the sound.

When letter pairs are introduced, students have key words to pair with the letters. The student reads the underlined letter pair first, then reads the whole word. The lessons always provide examples of words that include the target letter pair (should you forget what the letter pair sounds like in isolation).

After the student says all the letter sounds, have the student write the letter for the most recently introduced sound and other sounds that are not yet automatic. When you ask a student to write a letter, say the letter *sound*, not the letter name ("Now write the letter that says /aaa/.").

Letter Sounds Cards

If a student is not learning letter sounds at the rate the sounds are being introduced and reviewed in the lessons, you should add practice. You can do this by pairing each sound with the key word in the lessons. As noted earlier, if the classroom teacher uses different key words to teach letter sounds, substitute those in the tutoring lessons.

As tutor, you can also add practice in letter-sound correspondence by using the Letter Sounds Cards. For a few minutes at the beginning of a tutoring session, have the student practice a group of letters that are difficult for the student. The student points to each letter or letter pair, going first from letter to sound, then from sound to letter. If the student is having difficulty reading the ea letter pair, have the student point and say: ea, "leaf," /ea/ (letter names, key word, and letter sound). If the student is having difficulty spelling the letter pair, the student would point and say: "leaf," /ea/, ea (key word, letter sound, and letter names).

You may ask . . .

When I'm teaching the letters, does it matter if the student tells me the letter name or the letter sound?

The *Sound Partners* program focuses on letter-sound knowledge, which is critical for students learning to read. Many students who already know the names of the letters are not able to match each letter and its sound. Tutors work with their students on the letter sounds in the early lessons. It is very important that you yourself know the correct sound for each letter and model this for the student—for example, a quickly sounded /d/ and /p/ for these stop sounds, and not "duh" and "puh." It is most important that you model the correct short vowel sounds, as many children have difficulty discriminating between the /a/ and /e/ sounds, the /e/ and /i/ sounds, and the /o/ and /u/ sounds.

Segmenting

This activity teaches the student to separate words into individual phonemes. It is an auditory activity, and the student must learn to do it *without* looking at the word. Students learn to segment words into three and four phonemes. This activity can be very difficult for some students, but with repeated practice it can be mastered by all students. Model the skill for the student; a set of divided boxes is used as a visual cue. It is very important that during this activity you and the student stop between each sound and not blend sounds together as in the Word Reading section. The ability to segment words is particularly useful to children as they begin to write and spell. You should encourage students to first orally segment a word they have difficulty spelling.

After you say each word, the student should first repeat the word so you know the student heard it correctly. The task requires the student to point and say one sound for each box. You should correct the student if the sounds overlap (e.g., /m/ . . . *map*), and then model the correct response (/m/ /a/ /p/).

If the student needs assistance with four-phoneme segmenting with consonant blends, sound out the word slowly, say the sounds yourself, and have the student point to the boxes. If the student needs more assistance, write the letters above the boxes, then fade out these forms of assistance. Segmenting is an *auditory* (listening) task; the student should not be reading and should not see the words. He should be able to segment just by hearing the word. Cover the printed words if necessary.

You may ask . . .

Why is segmenting important?

The segmented boxes provide a concrete means of teaching children how to break words into individual phonemes. It helps make children aware that words are made up of separate sounds. They do this activity as they are also learning that each sound is associated with a letter of the alphabet or with a combination of letters. They build up to separating four-phoneme words that include initial and final consonant blends.

My student has just begun segmenting four-letter words with consonant blends in the sound boxes. Most of the time he can't do it—he can't seem to hear the inside consonant in a word like "sent." Is there anything I can do to help him?

One strategy is to tell the student, "I'll say the sounds and you point to the box each sound goes in." After the student is able to do this, switch roles and have the student say the sounds as you point. Finally, have the student point to the boxes, then say the sounds and point.

Another strategy that helps some students is to write the letters of the word above the box and have the student sound each one out and point to the appropriate box.

Once the student can segment with these aids, return to the unassisted segmenting task. Students must learn to segment words without printed letters, just by listening to the words. This skill enables them to spell words correctly.

Word Reading

For many students, learning to sound out words properly is the beginning of independent reading success. Once students master the letter sounds in a given word and can say the stretched-out sounds together quickly, they may master the sounding-out skill in ten or fewer lessons. Some students will have more difficulty identifying letter sounds, holding the sequence of sounds in memory, and running the sounds together so that they recognize the word. These students will need more practice in the sounding-out skill.

The lesson formats describe how to sound out words properly. Being able to sound out words is the most important skill *Sound Partners* tutors teach. Children should not progress to subsequent lessons until they have mastered sounding out. Whenever a student encounters a difficult decodable word in a text, you should scaffold or correct the student by asking the student to sound it out.

Model sounding out *without* stopping between sounds. Move immediately from one sound to the next (e.g., "sssaaammm," *not* /s/-/a/-/m/). You should really exaggerate *stretching* continuous sounds. Do not continue with lessons until the student can demonstrate how to use this strategy. Do not accept recognizing and reading a word by sight as a correct response when you begin to teach the sounding-out skill. The student must demonstrate the strategy in order to be able to decode new words. Sometimes it helps to describe this stretching out of sounds as "singing" or "humming" the sounds.

Sounding-Out Scaffolding

If a student cannot blend a three-phoneme word, like <u>bat</u>, do the following:

▶ Cover the last letter.

▶ Have the student blend the first two phonemes: "baaa."

▶ Then, have the student add the last phoneme: "baaat."

At the end of Word Reading, students practice spelling words they are learning to read. You dictate, and the student writes the words on a piece of paper or in a notebook. Choose words the student needs to practice. Include words with newly introduced sounds, with sounds the student needs to practice, and with sounds the student can spell successfully. Students should always reread the words they spell. When the student has difficulty spelling a word, encourage the student to segment the word into its sounds and then write the letters that match the sound. You can use large graph paper for this phoneme-to-grapheme mapping.

You may ask . . .

Is it important that the student not stop between the sounds when sounding out a word?

Sound Partners teaches students to blend the sounds together continuously to help them decode and identify unfamiliar words. If the student stops between the sounds, he will often not be able to hear and recognize the word he is decoding. That said, some students who have already learned in their classrooms to stop between each sound when blending have been able, through tutoring, to make sense of the words they were decoding in that manner. If the student is sounding out words successfully with this strategy, don't try to teach the student a new strategy that may just confuse the student.

Sight Words

Many words are not phonetically regular or cannot be sounded out with the limited skills early readers have. Some of these words (e.g., "of," "was," "they") occur very frequently in children's books and must be treated differently by the tutor and reader.

In the Sight Words section of the *Sound Partners* lessons, most irregular words are introduced before they are encountered in text. Introduce a new sight word by reading it and then asking the student to read the word, point to each letter, spell the word, and read the word again. While students are *not* told not to sound out these words (how would they know which words are which?), they are taught that some words sound out funny and need to be remembered. In fact, when young readers attempt to sound out irregular words they often get helpful clues about the word. These phonemic clues, along with memory and context, allow students to read these words. When correcting errors on irregular words, simply provide the correct word for the student and have the student reread it.

If a student has difficulty learning frequently used sight words (e.g., "the," "for," "to," and "said") make flash cards for these words. Explain to the student that these are words we read lots of times, so it is important to learn to read them quickly and easily.

Reading Long Words

Beginning in Lesson 61, students are introduced to multisyllable words and words with endings, prefixes, and suffixes. First, students practice reading compound words, and later they learn inflected words and words with affixes.

Compound Words

Cover part of the word and let the student read the uncovered part. Then do the same with the other part of the word. Next, ask the student to put the parts together. Later, the student covers part of the word herself.

Multisyllable Words

First, model breaking words into syllables. Then have the student practice reading words chunked into syllables. Finally, the student must break words into syllables and then read the whole word.

Magic -e-

Beginning in Lesson 46, students are introduced to the magic -e-rule: If a word has an e on the end, the middle vowel says its name and the e is quiet. First, the student learns to identify the middle letter (the vowel) and the long vowel sounds, and to notice if a word ends in e. Then the student identifies the names of the middle letters in a list of words. Finally, the student practices reading and discriminating words with and without a magic -e- ("cut" and "cute," "nap" and "nape").

The student is taught to identify and read magic -e- words in stages through sequenced instruction with lists of words.

Stage 1

Introduce the rule: "If a word has an <u>e</u> at the end, the middle vowel says its name, and the <u>e</u> is quiet." Help the student to find the middle letter (vowel) in words and to notice whether a word ends in <u>e</u>. Help the student to identify the sound of the middle letters.

Stage 2

Ask the student to read mixed lists of words, some with and some without a magic -e-. Correct the student, if necessary, by reminding the student of the rule.

Although you will often remind the student of the magic -e- rule, students are *not* expected to memorize/say the rule.

Encourage students to notice magic -e- words in the stories. Praise students (using *specific* praise) when you notice students correctly reading these words (in context) after students have recently learned the rule.

Word Endings

The lessons introduce common word endings. Teach an ending by pointing to an isolated word ending (e.g., -<u>ing</u>) and saying words with the ending. *Do not pronounce endings in isolation.* Then have the student look at an ending (e.g., -<u>s</u>) and say a word with the ending. The lessons provide practice in reading words with endings and do not attempt to teach spelling rules. The lessons teach the -<u>s</u>, -<u>ed</u>, -<u>ing</u>, and -<u>y</u> endings, with the goal that students be able to read words with these endings.

Pair Practice

This component (beginning in Lesson 43) provides another format for practicing letter-pair correspondences. There is considerable spelling-sound predictability in English at the letter-pair unit level. Dictate letter-pair sounds for the student to write and have the student read and spell both words and nonwords with letter pairs that have been introduced.

Correct by asking the student to say the letter-pair sound (for reading) or remember the letters that make the sound (for spelling). Have the student refer to the Letter Sounds Card, if needed, to retrieve letter-pair information.

Mini-Components

Mini-components that last for two to four lessons provide added phonics instruction. These only appear in certain lessons. A brief description of each mini-component follows.

Final <u>m</u> and <u>n</u> Blends (Lessons 43–46)

The letter sounds /m/ and /n/ are nasal sounds that are produced by air in the nasal cavity. It is difficult to hear these sounds when they occur in a final blend, due to coarticulation. You will help students

become aware of these sounds by contrasting word pairs, one with and one without a final nasal m or n blend.

Inside-Sound Spelling (Lessons 39–42)
Because many phonemes seem to disappear when they are coarticulated in words, you will offer students practice in recognizing these elusive phonemes by providing them with contrasting word pairs, one with and one without a consonant blend.

Spelling Similar Sounds (Lessons 49–51)
Students often confuse the spellings for words containing tr and ch because of coarticulation. The /r/ and /ch/ sounds are produced in a similar manner, and when the /t/ and /r/ sounds are coarticulated, the sound is made in the same part of the mouth as the /ch/ phoneme. You will provide students with practice reading and spelling word pairs that contrast the two pairs, which helps the student be more aware of the /r/ in tr blends.

Long u Sounds (Lessons 53–56)
In magic -e- words, the u may either sound like /oo/ as in tune or like /y-u/ as in cute. Students practice identifying which long u sound occurs in words. Students need to try both sounds when they are reading unfamiliar long u words.

Useful Word Chunks (Lessons 57–59)
It is helpful to teach the -igh and -ight families since they appear in many of the *Sound Partners* storybooks. Students should practice reading and spelling words in these families.

Double Consonants (Lessons 72–74)
You will teach the rule for words with double final consonants: If a single-syllable word with a short vowel ends in f, s, l, or z, the final letter is usually doubled. Students practice spelling single-syllable words (ending in f, s, l, or z) both with and without a short vowel.

Contraction Review (Lessons 95 and 99)
You will teach the students how to determine when and where apostrophes should appear in words. First, students read a list of contraction words in different word families. The students then practice the long way of saying each contraction (breaking it up into two words) and identify the missing letters in each contraction. Finally, the students practice spelling these words.

Book-Reading Instructions

After the first 15–20 minutes of hard work on the component reading skills during the first part of the lesson session, students and tutors alike enjoy applying those skills during the storybook reading. If the student has mastered sound identification, sounding out, and word lists, reading the story will be fun and rewarding. The lessons have been designed to require a minimum of instruction during book reading, and the activity affords practice in the component skills. Of course, students will make errors, and error correction is an important part of instruction.

The repeated reading of the storybooks in the lessons builds fluency (rate and accuracy). Students need lots of practice rereading familiar text to build confidence and success. Book reading guidelines— including time spent on reading, which books to read, how to read with the student, how to correct student errors, and two reading rules—are outlined below.

General Guidelines

With many students, you will be able to complete all of the lesson components before it's time to read books; this is obviously most desirable. However, book reading is a balancing act. If a student is struggling with the lesson content, she may not cover the entire lesson before it's time to read. In this case, she may not be able to read independently because she has not yet mastered all of the subskills that are assumed to have been taught prior to book reading.

You should do your best to cover as much of the lesson as possible prior to Book Reading. If need be, help the student read with echo or partner reading (see below). Schedule reading time during each 30-minute session, using the method that best matches the student's reading ability.

Some general guidelines:

1. Book Reading is the last activity in *each tutoring session*, beginning with Lesson 6. If a lesson is not completed and it is time for Book Reading (last 10–15 minutes of the tutoring session), have the student reread the book assigned to the most recently *completed* lesson.

   > **Example:** You are working with your student on the middle portion of Lesson 34, and you have reached the last 10 minutes of the tutoring session. Skip step 1 of the Book-Reading Steps (below), and have the student reread the book assigned to Lesson 33, *The Big Hat*. Then have the student reread other previously read books for the remaining time.

2. Time spent on Book Reading varies by lesson number. For the first half of the lesson sequence, you should spend 10 minutes reading at the end portion of each tutoring session (the second half of the lesson sequence requires 15 minutes of reading).

3. Try to *complete as many Book-Reading Steps* as possible. If a book has been assigned to multiple consecutive lessons (e.g., the book *Samantha* is assigned to four lessons, 67–70), skip step 2 of the Book-Reading Steps, and go from step 1 to step 3.

4. If you have time left over, and you have completed all Book-Reading Steps, begin the next lesson. This is likely to occur only in the early lessons when there are not as many books to read. There are also Supplementary Reading suggestions spaced sporadically throughout the lessons. Some titles for Supplementary Reading are noted in the lessons, and many more titles are listed in the Additional Supplementary Reading Scope and Sequence.

Book-Reading Time

Lessons	Minutes
6–49	10 minutes
50–100+	15 minutes

Book-Reading Steps

Step 1: Read the book assigned to the lesson twice, *if it is the first time the book appears in the lessons*. If it is the second, third, or fourth consecutive time the book appears in the lessons, read it through once and go to step 3 (e.g., *The Big Hat* is assigned to Lessons 32–33. Read *The Big Hat* twice for Lesson 32 but only once for Lesson 33).

Step 2: Read the previous lesson's book once.

Step 3: If there is time left, reread previously read books from earlier lessons.

Book-Reading Methods

Method	Definition
Independent	Student reads aloud by him or herself.
Partner	Student and tutor read aloud together.
Echo	Tutor reads one line of text aloud, and then student rereads same line. Repeat process throughout book.

Book-Reading Error Correction

When the student makes a reading error, isolate the difficult sounds in the word, and help the student blend the word. If it is a sight word, simply provide the correct word. Always have the student reread the entire sentence in which the word appears. This is important, so we will repeat it:

▶ Isolate the difficult portion/sounds in the word, direct the student to the portion, and help her sound out and/or blend the word. If the word is a sight word, simply provide the correct word.

▶ Have the student reread the corrected word and then the entire sentence with the word in context.

Book Reading: Two Rules

Students must follow two rules for storybook reading:

1. *Always* fingerpoint. There is an amazing difference in accuracy and fluency when early readers track each word with their finger when reading. Fingerpointing also lets you, the tutor, follow along. Many children resist this for some reason. Model by pointing for yourself when you read for your students.

2. *Reread* any sentence with an error, for added practice ("Let's read that again"). Correct *all* errors immediately by supplying the word (if it is a sight word or if it has not previously been taught) or by having the student sound out the word (when all sounds are known and/or the word has appeared in the lessons). After the student or tutor corrects an error, the student *always* returns to the beginning of the sentence and rereads. This procedure allows smoother reading for comprehension and extra practice on difficult words. Using this procedure consistently and positively helps student progress.

Book-Reading Discussion

Tutors should briefly discuss the book with students before, during, and after reading by asking the following or similar questions:

▶ What do you already know about (book topic)?

▶ What happened so far?

▶ What were the most important ideas?

▶ What do you think will happen next?

▶ Briefly, tell me the story in your own words.

You may ask . . .

My student refuses to fingerpoint when he reads.

One way to avoid this argument is to make it clear from the start that, "We fingerpoint when we read when we are together." If you've been inconsistent about this, you may be able to get your student to point with the eraser of his pencil. As a last resort, you can fingerpoint for the student, making sure that the student is following along as you point.

If a student reads accurately but very slowly, does it matter?

The ultimate goal of reading instruction is to enable the student to read fluently with comprehension of what she is reading. When a student reads very slowly, word by word, it is difficult for the student to get the meaning of the text, and the student becomes unmotivated to read. Once a student is beginning to blend and decode words accurately, you should encourage the student to read at a pace at which she gets the meaning of the text. You can check this by asking the student a question about the sentence or page the student just read. Then coax (but don't push or rush) the student to read a little bit faster by saying:

▶ "Now let's try reading the next page really smooth."

▶ "Can you try to read the next page a little bit quicker?"

▶ "Let's try to read this page like you were reading it to your little brother."

Why do children read well one day but not the next?

Many factors may account for a student's variable reading performance during tutoring. A first grader's attentiveness and alertness will influence reading. The tutoring setting may influence the student's desire to perform well on a particular day. If a story contains difficult, new letter sounds or blends that have been recently introduced, accuracy and fluency will decline. Finally, first graders often experience many childhood illnesses, and a student who has been out sick with a virus or chicken pox may take a few weeks to feel completely well again.

How can I encourage my student to read more carefully—so often it seems like he just isn't paying attention or trying?

Fingerpointing is one way to help beginning readers focus on the individual words in a story. If a student is just guessing at the words or making up his own story, cover the pictures in the story with an index card and ask the student to read without the illustrations. You can use a simple point system to reinforce the student for fingerpointing and for paying attention to the story.

Why does the student have to reread any sentence with an error?

In these lessons, one goal of story reading is to practice the decoding skills that are taught in the rest of the lesson. After the student shows you that he knows the letter sounds and sounding-out strategy, he applies those skills in a story carefully chosen so that he will have to use those skills. If a student comes across a word that he doesn't know, he uses the strategies he has been taught, and if he still doesn't know the word, you will provide it. By rereading the sentence, the student gets more practice reading a difficult word and also regains the sense of the sentence. After the student rereads the sentence, give specific praise for how much he improved his speed or accuracy.

Why aren't there more comprehension activities in the program?

Sound Partners is carefully designed to teach the lowest 20% of first graders a critical set of early reading skills. It is also designed to be used by tutors in a valuable half-hour block of classroom time. We had to make difficult choices about what to include in the lessons. We encourage you to ask comprehension questions during the Book-Reading Time. We also assume that each student's classroom teacher is working on comprehension during classroom reading instruction and that comprehension will become a bigger emphasis in the student's reading instruction after early reading skills are mastered.

Vocabulary Instruction

Although there is not time for extended vocabulary instruction during a *Sound Partners* session, you can address vocabulary incidentally.

This will become easier as you gain experience with the lessons. Once you become familiar with the lessons and comfortable using them, you will have time to notice when your student needs incidental vocabulary instruction. You won't be able to offer extended vocabulary instruction, but you will be able to provide brief vocabulary help. Vocabulary help may be needed if your student isn't able to find the correct pronunciation for a word. Or you may ask a question to check comprehension and find that the student does not know the meaning of a word. You should then add brief vocabulary instruction.

▶ **Choose** words that are important. These are words that are used frequently or are important to understanding a particular story.

▶ **Tell** the meaning of the word in everyday language. Try to wrap an example into your definition.

  For example, "To *squirm* is to wriggle and be uncomfortable. John didn't do his homework and he started to *squirm* when the teacher started calling on the class for their answers."

▶ **Ask** the student to use the word.

  For example, "Tell me something about your life, and use the word *inspire*."

▶ **Involve** the student in the word. Ask the student a question that uses the word.

  For example, for the word *stern*: "How might your teacher feel if she is looking *stern*?

  For example, for the word *perky*: "If you were feeling *perky*, how would you look? Dragging your feet with your head hung down? Crying and sad? Walking quickly and looking happy and bright-eyed?"

Mastery Tests

Every ten lessons, you should administer a short test (spaced throughout the lessons; Recording Sheets are available in the Appendix) to assess the student's mastery of the concepts being taught. The tests assess student mastery of letter sounds, word reading, and spelling. Each Mastery Test includes a Student Recording Sheet and a Tester Recording Sheet. The Student Recording Sheet includes the words that the student reads. The Tester Recording Sheet includes the directions, the sounds and words to dictate for spelling, and the scoring section. The scoring section also includes instructions for added review, based on the student's performance.

Mastery Tests can also be used to place a student in the lessons. For example, if a student already knows some letter sounds and has beginning sound-blending skills, you can use the Mastery Test to place the student at an appropriate level.

It is best if you do not test your own student, but have another tutor do the testing. However, this can be difficult to arrange. And, unlike normal lesson time, you should not provide feedback or assistance when administering the Mastery Tests.

Error Correction and Specific Praise

Remember that immediate, specific, and relevant feedback is a strong teacher. Here are some guidelines for error correction and specific praise.

Error Correction—Draw the student's attention to an error in a way that helps her see the nature of the mistake, then have the student correct the response and reread the word or sentence. If necessary, model the correct response, and then have the student repeat. *Example: Student says "cat" when the word is "cot." Direct student to the middle sound and say, "What's the sound?" If the student says /o/, ask the student to reread the word again, fast. If the student does not know the sound, model /o/ for the student, and have the student repeat.*

Specific Praise—Tell students *immediately* when they are doing a good job. Tell them *specifically* what they are doing well, and talk about aspects of the task that are important. Specific praise examples are given below.

Student Action	Tutor Says:
Student correctly says the /ea/ letter-pair sound in "beak" as /eeee/.	*"That's right, ea says /ee/."*
Student used finger to point while reading (after several reminders).	*"I like the way you are using your finger to keep your place—that works very well."*
Student sounds out a difficult word, "drink."	*"You got all of the sounds in 'drink' just right!"*
Student spells words in her writing that you can figure out.	*"Good job spelling the words like they sound."*
Student applies a new or difficult rule correctly (e.g., correctly reads the word "mate.")	*"Terrific! You remembered the magic -e- rule for that word."*
Student rereads a difficult sentence independently.	*"I like the way you read that again smoothly. That is how good readers get even better."*
Student reads smoothly and with expression.	*"Good reading with lots of expression—it was fun to listen."*
Student accurately segments the word "bags" as /b/-/a/-/g/-/s/.	*"Good hearing each sound in the word and putting it in a box."*
Student correctly finds the letters in a letter pair and says the sound.	*"You really know that pair! You read all of the words with that pair perfectly."*
Student spells new words with the /ou/ pair.	*"I like how you spelled the words 'out' and 'shout.' You are really thinking about that pair. Good work."*

Student Behavior Management

Set Ground Rules—If needed, establish behavioral ground rules for your student during your tutoring sessions. State these rules when you first begin tutoring. Make the rules simple and specific. Be sure you and your student can tell whether she is following the rules. For example:

> **Don't say:** *"Let's work together well this year."*
>
> **Do say:** *"During tutoring, we sit in our chairs with our feet on the floor. It's my job to help you, and your job to listen and follow my directions."*

▶ **Avoid negative comments** such as "No, that's not right." If the student's response is incorrect, either encourage the student to self-correct or model the correct response for the student (and then have the student reread).

▶ **Do praise your student**, but use praise only when your student has earned it. Otherwise, praise will lose its value to the student.

▶ **Always be specific with praise.** Say what it is you are praising the student for (see previous examples of specific praise).

Keep Pace—Maintain a brisk pace. Redirect and keep going when a student's talk or behavior is off-task. Don't become engaged in unrelated conversation; save this for the walk back to the classroom.

Be Consistent—Always require fingerpointing, rereading, and applying the target strategy.

When All Else Fails—If the student refuses to cooperate after you have tried to redirect him to the lesson, return the student to class and seek further suggestions from the designated supervisor (e.g., tutor trainer, classroom teacher, or school principal).

Things to Remember

▶ **Follow *Sound Partners* lessons carefully.**

Each component has been designed and field-tested to teach your students specific skills they need to become good readers. Make sure you are providing the best instruction you can to help them become successful readers by consistently following all directions shown in the lessons. Work through the lessons in sequence and don't skip or omit sections. Care in implementing the lessons is the strongest predictor of student outcomes.

▶ **Use the full 30 minutes of instruction.**

Students have a great deal of material to cover to reach grade level. Their time in school is extremely valuable. Use the full 30 minutes to provide instruction in specific reading skills. Don't allow students to fall farther behind because of missed classroom time and poor tutoring instruction!

▶ **Track student attendance and progress.**

An Attendance/Lesson Completion Form is provided in the Appendix. Use it to log tutor sessions and lesson completion. In addition to Mastery Test results, you may also find it useful to share with classroom teachers completed *Sound Partners* Progress Reports, also in the Appendix, which correlate to the numbered Mastery Tests.

▶ **Use specific praise.**

Students need feedback to improve their reading skills and stay motivated. Give immediate, specific praise when your students have earned it.

▶ **Correct all errors immediately and consistently.**

Make note of specific error types and add practice in areas of weakness. Make sure the students always repeat the correct response after self-correcting or after you model the correct response. Finally, give students more practice in new or difficult strategies (e.g., the magic -e- rule).

▶ **Maintain a brisk pace.**

With a brisk pace, students will better attend to the material. They will not have any time to be off-task. Additionally, students will cover more lessons, and be more likely to catch up with their classmates on reading skills.

▶ **Refresh your knowledge of *Sound Partners* procedures.**

Test yourself periodically using the Tutor Self-Check Quiz on page 32.

▶ **Good instruction is the most valuable gift you can offer your student.**

The most caring thing you can do is to help your students improve their reading skills. Reading is the most important academic skill your students need.

Tutor Self-Check Quiz

1. What are the sounds of these letters and letter pairs?

e	b	a	o	u	al	ow	ir
r	y	i	d	g	ou	ea	oo
h	k	l	c	w	oa	er	ew

2. What key words do you use for letter sounds?

3. What can you do to help your student if he has difficulty segmenting words by pointing to the boxes in the lesson?

4. What would you say if your student cannot read a word in her storybook?

5. What are the two rules that students must always follow during storybook reading?

6. Your student has had difficulty identifying the last sound in a word. Today he has read the word "sag" correctly for the first time. What would be an effective comment to praise him?

7. How should you use the Letter Sounds Cards?

8. How do you decide which words from the Word Reading lesson component to have your student spell?

9. How do you help your student read a multisyllable or compound word?

10. How would you introduce your student to a sight word, like the word "said"?

11. Name two things you would do if your student has difficulty discriminating the short /a/ and /e/ sounds?

12. What would you say if your student has trouble spelling one of the words that you dictate, like "rug"?

13. Which of these letters are stop sounds and which are continuous sounds?

    n a h g b e p s m d t

14. What should you do with items (letters, letter pairs, and words) that appear in boxes in the lessons?

15. What should your student be doing when you ask her to segment a word?

16. How do you use the word-ending boxes when you teach word endings?

Key to Tutor Self-Check Quiz

1. Use an audiotape if needed to check the letter sounds.

2. Use the lesson key words that match the Letter Sounds Cards—unless you know that your student's classroom teacher uses a different set of key words. In that case, use the key words that your student's classroom is using.

3. If your student can't segment by putting one sound in each box, you can:
   a. Say the sounds in the word and have the student point as you say each sound, or
   b. Model by pointing and saying the sounds, then have the student repeat.

4. If your student can't read a word in the story:
   a. Ask her to sound it out,
   b. Ask the student what the first sound is, then ask her to sound out the word,
   c. Help the student by starting to sound out the word, then letting the student complete, or
   d. If the word is a sight word or if the student still can't sound out a word containing previously taught sounds, tell the student the word and then have her repeat it and reread the sentence.

5. Two rules students must always follow are:
   a. Fingerpointing when reading words or text, and
   b. Rereading the sentence if they make an error.

6. Good specific praise would be: "You read the last sound, /g/, in that word exactly right!"

7. Use the Letter Sounds Cards to review sounds your student still needs to practice. Practice several rows of sounds for five minutes at the beginning of the session. Keep the Letter Sounds Cards out for the student to see and refer to them for both reading and spelling. Remind the student to refer to the cards when needed.

8. Choose the spelling words that your student has had the most difficulty reading correctly. You can also choose words that include elements that have been most recently taught in the lessons.

9. Have your student say the word by breaking it into parts. Cover one part of the word while the student reads the first chunk/syllable. Then uncover more of the word for the student to read.

10. Introduce each new sight word by telling the student the word. *Example: "This word is 'said.' You read it. Now spell it. Now read it again."*

11. If your student confuses two vowel sounds, you can:
    a. Remind the student of the key words for each vowel,
    b. Model each vowel sound very clearly/distinctly for the student, or
    c. Tell the student to notice the shape of your mouth/lips when you say each vowel sound.

12. If your student has trouble spelling a word, you can:
    a. Tell the student to sound out the word, and spell each sound he hears,
    b. Ask your student what each sound is (*Example: "What is the first sound in 'rug'? And what is the next/middle sound in 'rug'? And what is the next/last sound 'rug'?"*),
    c. Sound out the word slowly for the student while he writes the sounds, or
    d. Be sure to have the student reread each word he has written.

13. Stop sounds are: h, g, b, p, d, and t. Continuous sounds are: n, a, e, s, and m.

14. The lessons are designed so that all new letter sounds and pairs and sight words appear in a box. This means you will introduce and model these new sounds and words before you ask the student to read them.

15. Your student should be listening to you say the word. Segmenting is a listening task, not a reading task. Therefore, it is very important that your student not see the printed word you ask her to segment. Students need to learn to segment words by just listening to them and breaking them into the individual sounds. Have the student say the word before segmenting, and repeat the word after segmenting.

16. You point to the box with the word ending and say: "I can say _____ word with this ending." Then point to the box and say the example word with the ending. Do not try to read/pronounce the ending in isolation, as the sound of an ending depends on the word to which it is attached (e.g., the **-ed** ending may sound like "d" or like "t" depending on the root word). You may want to tell your student that some endings, like **-s** and **-ed**, sound different at the ends of different words.

Bibliography

Carnine, D., Silbert, J., & Kame'enui, E. J. (1990). Direct instruction reading. Englewood Cliffs, NJ: Prentice-Hall.

Sound Partners Reading Books

All books are published by Scholastic.

Bob Books, written by Bobby Lynn Maslen and illustrated by John Maslen, are a wonderful series of boxed, phonics-based storybooks for beginning readers.

Bob Books: First! (Level A, Set 1) (1976, rev. 2000)

Mat

Sam

Dot

Mac

Dot and the Dog

Dot and Mit

Jig and Mag

Muff and Ruff

10 Cut Ups

Peg and Ted

Lad and the Fat Cat

The Vet

Bob Books: Fun! (Level A, Set 2) (1999)

Fun in the Sun

Up Pup

Pip and Pog

The Big Hat

Bow Wow

Go Bus

The Red Hen

Sox the Fox

The Sad Cat

Rub a Dub

OK Kids

0 to 10

Bob Books: Plus! (Level B, Set 1) (1996)

Kittens

Floppy Mop

Summer

Lolly Pops

The Red Car

Frogs

Funny Bunny

Bed Bugs

Bob Books: Pals! (Level B, Set 2) (1987, rev. 2000)

Ten Men

Bump

The Swimmers

Cat and Mouse

Max and the Tom Cats

Willy's Wish

Jumper and the Clown

Samantha

Bob Books: Wow! (Level C, Set 1) (1987, rev. 2000)

Bud's Nap

The Game

Joe's Toe

The Picnic

The King

The Train

Chickens

The Visit

The Class Trip (1999) by Grace Maccarone

Mice and Beans (2005) by Pam Muñoz Ryan

Poppleton and Friends (1998) by Cynthia Rylant

Additional Supplementary Reading Books

Metropolitan Teaching and Learning Leveled Books: Fiction Series
available from Cambium Learning Web Store:
http://store.cambiumlearning.com

Phonics Funnies Storybooks available from Voyager Sopris Learning,
Longmont, CO.

Primary Phonics books available from Educator's Publishing Service,
Cambridge, MA.

Lesson Component Scope and Sequence

Sound Partners

COMPONENTS	LESSONS									
	1	2	3	4	5	6	7	8	9	10
New Letter Sounds/ Pairs	a, m	s	t	Review	c	d	n	o	Review	h
Say the Sounds (and Write Sounds)	a, [m]	a, m, [s]	a, m, s, [t]	a, m, s, t	a, [c], m, s, t	a, c, [d], m, s, t	a, c, d, m, [n], s, t	a, c, d, m, n, [o], s, t	a, c, d, m, n, o, s, t	a, c, d, [h], m, n, o, s, t
Segmenting	3-part	3-part	3-part	3-part	3-part	3-part	3-part	3-part	3-part	3-part
Word Reading (and Spelling)*	am	Sam	at, mat, sat, tam	Review	Cam, cat, Mac	cad, mad, sad, Tad	ad, and, Dan, tan	cot, dad, Dot, mom, nod, not, on, sod, Tom	con	cod, had, ham, hat, hot
Book Reading						*Mat* Bob Books A-1	*Mat* Bob Books A-1		*Sam* Bob Books A-1	*Sam* Bob Books A-1

*Only newly introduced words listed.

Lesson Component Scope and Sequence

LESSONS

COMPONENTS	11	12	13	14	15	16	17	18	19	20
New Letter Sounds/ Pairs	g	r	b	Review	i	Review	Review	p	w	j
Say the Sounds (and Write Sounds)	a, c, d, g , h, m, n, o, s, t	a, c, d, g, h, m, n, o, r , s, t	a, b , c, d, g, h, m, n, o, r, s, t	a, b, c, g, h, m, n, o, r, t	a, b, c, g, h, i , m, n, o, r, s	a, b, c, d, g, i, m, n, o, r, t	a, b, c, d, g, h, i, m, n, o, r, s, t	a, b, c, d, g, h, i, n, o, p , r	a, b, c, d, h, i, o, p, t, w	a, b, d, g, i, j , m, n, p, r, s, w
Segmenting	3-part	3-part	3-part	3-part	3-part	3-part	3-part	3-part	3-part	3-part
Word Reading (and Spelling)*	cog, got, nag, sag, tag	hog, Nat, rag, ran, rat	bag, ban, bat, bog, cab, mob, nab, sob	bad, Mag	bin, dig, dim, hit, it, sit, tin	big, can, dab, hid, rid, rig	did, dog, Mit	bop, dip, hop, map, mop, nap, pan, pig, pin, pit, pot, ram, rap, rip	cap, pad, pat, wag, wig, win, wit	jam, jig, Jim, job, jog, jot
Sight Words*	a, The	Review	in	as, has	Review	his, is	isn't	of	you	to
Book Reading	*Sam* Bob Books A-1	*Dot* Bob Books A-1	*Dot and Mit* Bob Books A-1	*Mac* Bob Books A-1		*Dot and the Dog* Bob Books A-1		*Dot and Mit* Bob Books A-1		*Jig and Mag* Bob Books A-1

*Only newly introduced words listed.

Sound Partners

Lesson Component Scope and Sequence

Sound Partners

COMPONENTS	LESSONS									
	21	22	23	24	25	26	27	28	29	30
New Letter Sounds/ Pairs	u	Review	f	Review	e	Review	th	k	l	x
Say the Sounds (and Write Sounds)	a, b, d, h, i, j, n, p, r, [u], w	a, d, h, i, j, n, p, r, u, w	b, [f], i, j, n, p, r, s, u, w	a, d, f, g, i, j, p, r, s, t, u, w	a, b, d, [e], f, j, m, n, t, u, w	b, c, d, e, f, j, p, r, s, t, u	a, b, e, f, h, i, o, r, t, u, w, [th]	a, e, f, g, j, [k], n, p, t, u, th	d, e, f, g, i, [l], k, r, w, th	d, e, f, g, j, k, l, o, p, u, [x], th
Segmenting	3-part	3-part	3-part	3-part	3-part	4-part	4-part	4-part	4-part	4-part
Word Reading (and Spelling)*	bud, bug, cup, cut, dud, hug, jig, jut, pup, rib, up	bun, rim, rub, run	fad, fan, fat, fig, fin, fit, fun, Muff, Ruff	fog, huff, puff, rot	fed, men, pet, red, rug, tug, wet	dug, hen, jet, nut, sap, tip	bath, bib, get, net, path, pen, rut, that, then, thin	dub, gum, keg, kid, Kim, Kip, kit, than, this	fell, let, lid, log, lop, lot, mill, pill	box, fix, fox, mix, set, six
Sight Words*	Review	Review	for, or	can't, didn't	come, some	into	were	be, he, me, we	said	it's, let's
Word Endings	[s]	s	s	s						
Book Reading	Jig and Mag Bob Books A-1		Muff and Ruff Bob Books A-1		10 Cut Ups Bob Books A-1		Peg and Ted Bob Books A-1		Lad and the Fat Cat Bob Books A-1	
Supplementary Reading					Fun in the Sun Bob Books A-1		Up Pup Bob Books A-1		Pip and Pog Bob Books A-1	

*Only newly introduced words listed.

Lesson Component Scope and Sequence

Sound Partners

LESSONS

COMPONENTS	31	32	33	34	35	36	37	38	39	40
New Letter Sounds/Pairs	Review	v	y	z	sh	Review	ch	Review	Review	wh
Say the Sounds (and Write Sounds)	a, c, e, f, i, k, l, o, s, t, u, x, th	a, b, e, h, i, j, u, k, l, v, x, th	a, e, i, k, l, n, s, t, v, x, y, th	e, i, l, o, r, t, u, v, x, y, z, th	d, e, f, i, k, o, p, u, v, x, y, z, sh	a, c, e, h, l, o, s, t, u, v, w, y, z, sh	b, h, i, j, o, u, v, x, y, z, ch, sh	e, h, i, j, l, n, t, u, y, z, ch, sh	a, e, g, i, l, o, r, u, v, x, y, z, ch, sh	d, e, k, l, n, t, x, y, z, ch, th, wh
Segmenting	4-part	4-part	4-part	4-part	4-part	4-part	4-part			
Word Reading (and Spelling)*	lip, met, Ned, nub	lug, van, vat, vet, vex	yak, yap, yen, yes, yet, yup	fax, fizz, fuzz, jazz, leg, sip, zam, zap, zig, zip	band, bus, buzz, fish, lag, mash, rash, shed, shop, web	bash, dish, hand, land, lash, math, sand, shin, shot	bent, chat, chin, chip, chop, rich, sent, such, tent	dash, sham, shut, wish	best, blob, clip, flag, flip, nest, ship, slum, stop, west	hush, wham, when, whim, whip
Inside-Sound Spelling									✓ starts	✓
Sight Words*	was	they	I, I'll, I'm	all	Review	there	you'll	what, what's	Review	saw
Word Endings										
Book Reading	Lad and the Fat Cat Bob Books A-1	The Big Hat Bob Books A-2		The Vet Bob Books A-1		Bow-Wow Bob Books A-2		Ten Men Bob Books B-2	Ten Men Bob Books B-2	The Red Hen Bob Books A-2
Supplementary Reading									Go Bus Bob Books A-2	

*Only newly introduced words listed.

Lesson Component Scope and Sequence

LESSONS

COMPONENTS	41	42	43	44	45	46	47	48	49	50
New Letter Sounds/ Pairs	Review	Review	qu, fl, sk, sl	Review	er	sw	ee, st	ck	ou, tr	ue
Say the Sounds (and Write Sounds)	a, c, g, i, l, o, r, y, z, ch, sh, wh	c, d, e, i, l, o, p, u, v, w, x, y, ch, sh, wh	b, f, g, l, p, x, y, ch, [fl], [qu], [sk], [sl], th, wh	a, e, f, i, v, w, y, ch, fl, qu, sh, sk, sl, th, wh	a, b, h, j, l, o, u, y, z, ch, [er] qu, sk, wh	h, i, n, u, w, ch, er, fl, qu, sh, sk, sl, [sw], wh	g, i, l, p, r, x, z, ch, [ee], er, qu, [st], sw	a, d, e, h, o, p, ch, [ck], ee, er, qu, sh, sl, st, sw, wh	c, l, u, v, w, ch, ck, ee, er, [ou], sw, [tr]	j, t, y, ck, ee, er, ou, qu, sw, tr, [ue], wh
Word Reading (and Spelling)*	chap, gosh, much, mush, plan, plug, rent, shell, stag, with	lump, pump, shim, shod, step, stub, wax	chipped, flash, pumped, quit, quiz, skims, slash, task	chaps, chimp, skid, skips, them, thud	Bert, bumper, chill, crunched, faster, fern, helper, her, hunter, letter, robin, stern	ask, herder, mask, slipper, slump, stands, swims, swish, whiz	cheeks, feed, feel, glee, lifted, need, sheen, sleep, steel, steep, stone, sweeps, went	bee, chilly, feet, free, heel, lock, luck, quack, queen, quick, rancher	couch, hound, licked, limps, ouch, outer, round, rusty, shouted, south, straps, tricked, trout	blue, cloudy, clue, coffee, deeper, due, glue, ground, pouch, sifter, sixteen, thunder
Sight Words*	over	Review	she, she's	Review	Review	want	by, my	Review	house, mouse	Review
Inside-Sound Spelling	✓	✓								
Spelling Similar Sounds									[ch], [tr]	ch, tr
Magic -e-						✓starts	✓	✓	✓	✓
Word Endings		[ed] with /t/ sound	[ed] with /d/ sound	[ed] with /ed/ sound	ed (all)	[y]	y	y	✓	y
Final m and n Blends			✓ starts	✓	✓					
Pair Practice			✓ starts	✓	✓	✓	✓	✓	✓	✓
Book Reading	*Sox the Fox* Bob Books A-2	*Kittens* Bob Books B-1		*Rub a Dub* Bob Books A-2		*Bump* Bob Books B-2		*The Swimmers* Bob Books B-2		*Summer* Bob Books B-1
Supplementary Reading		*The Sad Cat* Bob Books A-2		*OK Kids* Bob Books A-2		*0-10* Bob Books A-2		*Floppy Mop* Bob Books B-1		*Lolly Pops* Bob Books B-1

*Only newly introduced words listed.

Lesson Component Scope and Sequence

Sound Partners

LESSONS

COMPONENTS	51	52	53	54	55	56	57	58	59	60
New Letter Sounds/Pairs	ew	Review	-y /ī/	Review	ar	Review	Review	ow	Review	al
Say the Sounds (and Write Sounds)	l, n, ck, ee, er, [ew], ou, qu, sl, sk, ue	ch, ck, ee, er, ew, ou, qu, sh, th, ue, wh	ck, er, ew, ou, qu, th, ue, [-y]	ch, ck, ee, er, ew, ou, qu, sh, ue, wh, -y	[ar], ck, ee, er, ew, ou, wh, -y	ar, ch, ck, ee, er, ew, ou, sh, th, wh, -y	ar, ch, ck, fl, ee, ew, [gr], ou, qu, sh, [sn], th, tr	ar, ck, ee, ew, ou, [ow], ue, -y	ar, ck, er, ew, gr, ou, ow, ue	[al], ar, ck, ee, ew, ou, ow, ue, wh
Word Reading (and Spelling)*	cloud, crew, dew, drew, found, new, our, out, sound, stew, teeth, weeds	flew, flop, flour, grew, quacks, slam, slap, snap, true, wheels	cry, dry, my, newer, shy, sky, try	chew, litter, loud, newest, rounder, supply, track	barn, hard, slick, tart, white, why, yarn	darker, grime, jar, market, parking, same, scar, slouch, start, threw, whine	flicker, green, grin, outing, sharp, snack, snout, stewing	arm, army, artist, brow, chart, chow, flower, plow, power, spark, started, wow	arch, ark, barking, charm, how, howl, shower, starter, tower	ball, brighter, calm, crowd, farmer, harp, high, now, salty, stall
Sight Words*	any, many	head	knew	know	have	Review	one, two	live	very	says
Spelling Similar Sounds	ch, tr									
Useful Word Chunks							[igh]	[ight]	Review	
Magic -e-		✓	✓	✓	✓	✓	✓	✓	✓	✓
Word Endings					[ing]	ing	y			ing
Long u Sounds			✓ starts	✓	✓	✓				
Pair Practice	✓	✓	✓	✓	✓	✓	✓ nonwords	✓ nonwords	✓ nonwords	✓ nonwords
Book Reading	*Summer* Bob Books B-1	*Cat and Mouse* Bob Books B-2		*Bud's Nap* Bob Books C-1		*The Red Car* Bob Books B-1		*Max and the Tom Cats* Bob Books B-2		*Willy's Wish* Bob Books B-2
Supplementary Reading	*Lolly Pops* Bob Books B-1									*Frogs* Bob Books B-1

*Only newly introduced words listed.

Lesson Component Scope and Sequence

Sound Partners

LESSONS

COMPONENTS	61	62	63	64	65	66	67	68	69	70
New Letter Sounds/ Pairs	Review	ay	Review	oo/oo	Review	oa	Review	ai	Review	ea
Say the Sounds (and Write Sounds)	al, ar, ee, er, ew, ou, ow, ue	al, ar, [ay], ew, ow	al, ar, ay, er, ew, ou, ow, th, ue	ar, ay, er, ew, [oo/oo], ou, ow, ue	al, ar, ay, ch, er, ee, ew, oo/oo, ou, ow, qu, sh, th, ue, wh	al, ay, [oa], oo/ oo, ow	al, ay, ew, oa, oo/oo, ou	[ai], ar, ay, er, ew, oa, oo, ou	ai, al, ar, ay, ee, er, ew, oa, oo, ou, ow, ue	ai, al, ay, [ea] ee, oa, oo
Word Reading (and Spelling)*	archer, ballgame, bright, brown, carpet, outfit, outside, scald, sheets, sparkler, sunshine, taller	clay, daytime, highest, marker, payday, pinball, play, smart, stray, target	always, frighten, intern, owl, perky, playground, skate, sprayed, staying, sticky, thing	boots, brewing, cartoons, clerk, farming, hook, mighty, room, shook, Sue, tar, troops	charts, crook, frowning, harsh, hood, layer, mark, quicker, thick, tighten, took, tooth	floated, lighter, malted, roasted, slight, soapy, toasty, wallet	bars, cooled, foamy, lumpy, mushy, pray, right, stamp, stood, swaying, toasted	days, failed, jail, mail, mermaid, paid, plain, rain, sailing, temper, waiting, way	away, brain, claim, flight, frogs, gray, noon, painted, stain, strainer, tools, trail	beans, dealer, heated, lean, meanest, painter, sealed, slightly, team, trailer, train, tray, treated, yeast
Sight Words*	Review	don't	Review	their	we'll, we've	who	eyes, from	are, aren't	go, no, so	find, kind
Reading Long Words	✓ start	✓	✓	✓	✓	✓	✓	✓	✓	✓
Magic -e-	✓	✓	✓	✓						
Word Endings					Review		Review			
Pair Practice	✓ nonwords									
Book Reading	Willy's Wish Bob Books B-2	Funny Bunny Bob Books B-1		Jumper and the Clown Bob Books B-2				Samantha Bob Books B-2		

*Only newly introduced words listed.

Lesson Component Scope and Sequence

Sound Partners

LESSONS

COMPONENTS	71	72	73	74	75	76	77	78	79	80
New Letter Sounds/ Pairs	Review	ir	Review	Review	kn	wr	Review	-ng	Review	-nk
Say the Sounds (and Write Sounds)	ai, ay, ea, ee, oa, oo, ou	ay, ea, ee, $\boxed{\text{ir}}$, oa, oo, ou, ow	ai, ea, ee, er, ir, oo, ou, ow, ue	ai, al, ar, ay, ch, ea, ee, er, ew, ir, oa, oo, qu, sh, ue, wh	knife, knee, kneel, knelt, knight, knit, knob, knock, knot	wrap, wreath, wrench, wrist, write, wrote	knead, knitting, knotted, wreck, wring	banging, bring, clanging, ding, fangs, gang, hanging, long, lungs, ring, sing, song, swing, stringy, things	hanger, long, ringing, sang, strong, stung, swing, wings	honk, ink, junk, mink, pink, stink, tanker, sinking, yanked
Word Reading (and Spelling)*	beater, cheat, deep, healing, meets, nailing, reads, street, treats, wheat	birch, birth, boats, dirt, fir, first, girls, owls, peach, peek, sir, steaming, stir	birds, growl, shampoo, shirt, sneak, squirm, thirsty, whirl	booklet, choke, coasters, march, shine, skirt, toad, trash, walrus, while	beast, doorknob, kicked, knead, knits, knotty, marsh, penknife, saint, scarf, stout	chirps, east, knapsack, kneecap, rooster, shark, shipwreck, twisted, unwrap, waist, write	croak, kneepad, knock, smirk, snail, swirl, third, wrong	brightly, chained, fainted, freeway, mouth, reaching, showers, slang, slingshot, slouching, string, sung, twirl	brings, clanging, daylight, falling, gaining, loudest, pleated, reached, rounded, trailing	blink, charcoal, coach, hunk, shrunk, Spain, spool, springs, squirt, stinking, tattoo, thanks, trunk
Sight Words*	both	where	Review	Review	Review	talk, walk	Review	because	put	four, your
Reading Long Words	✓	✓ starts								
Double Consonants			✓	✓						
Book Reading	*The Class Trip* Scholastic Books		*The Game* Bob Books C-1			*Mice and Beans* Scholastic Books		*Joe's Toe* Bob Books C-1		*The Picnic* Bob Books C-1

*Only newly introduced words listed.

Lesson Component Scope and Sequence

COMPONENTS	LESSONS									
	81	82	83	84	85	86	87	88	89	90
New Letter Sounds/ Pairs	Review	c /s/	g /j/	Review	Review	or	Review	aw	Review	Review
Say the Sounds (and Write Sounds)	blink, bonk, plank, spring, think, wrapper	cell, cellar, cent, center, cinder, circus, face, fancy, ice, Pacific, pencil, place	age, energy, gelatin, gem, gently, germ, ginger, gym, huge, large, page, rage	lace, rice	central, Cindy, price, spice	border, cork, for, forbid, forest, morning, normal, orbit, order, pork, sorts, sport	boring, corner, dormitory, florist, glory, horn, hornet, ordering, stork, shorter	awful, awkward, claw, crawl, gawk, lawn, outlaw, paws, raw, seesaw, shawl, straw	brawny, dawn, hawk, paws, saw, sawmill, yawning	cigar, skunk, thorn
Word Reading (and Spelling)*	clank, clink, headstrong, meantime, nightmare, sour, stream	acid, bringing, crosswalk, flashlight, honk, ice cream, knickers, offside, painting, pencil, pounding, rocket, sticking, stinger	banker, checkbook, energy, face, gerbil, nightgown, rocks, slice, stage, staff, stiffer	ace, fence	canter, mice, pigpen, slicker, whirling	corn, foghorn, forty, hang, hornpipe, lucky, popcorn, shock, shortest, sorting, stem, sticker, stork, story	bricks, cornhusk, forks, seaport, shorthand, shouting, snoring, streaky, strike	cheating, checkers, crawling, drawing, flickers, glide, glory, jaws, jawbone, jigsaw, meaty, playing, sprayer	awful, jaywalk, mainstream, north, organ, plywood, port, short, Sunday, torn, yucky	drain, gently, knockout, pocket, stuffy, thawing, written
Sight Words*	Review	do	move	Review	friend	sure	little	shiny	again	Review
Reading Long Words									✓	✓
Book Reading	The Picnic Bob Books C-1		Bed Bugs Bob Books B-1		The King, Part I Bob Books C-1		The King, Part II Bob Books C-1		The Train Bob Books C-1	

*Only newly introduced words listed.

Lesson Component Scope and Sequence

Sound Partners

LESSONS

COMPONENTS	91	92	93	94	95	96	97	98	99	100
New Letter Sounds/Pairs	-le	be-, de-, pre-, re-	-tion, -sion	Review	ur	Review	Review	ey	Review	oi, oy
Say the Sounds (and Write Sounds)	angle, ankle, buckle, circle, dribble, gentle, shuffle, simple, tickle	begin, belong, defend, detect, pretend, prevent, repay, retell, return	action, direction, election, fraction, friction, mansion, mission, section, subtraction, suction, tension, vision	betray, decision, detach, knuckle, mention, retire	burn, burst, church, disturb, fur, hurt, purr, surf, turn	blurry, burp, churn, nurse, turning	aw, be-, de-, ir, kn, -le, -ng, -nk, or, pre-, re-, -sion, -tion, ur, wr	alley, donkey, hockey, honey, key, kidney, money, turkey, valley		boil, coins, enjoy, joins, joy, moist, noisy, pointed, royal, soil, soy, spoiling, toys, voice
Word Reading (and Spelling)*	corks, cricket, crinkle, dimple, fangs, feast, jacket, pluck, singer, stumble, thimble, thorny	began, below, beside, between, border, decay, delight, detach, portray, predict, remote, reply, request, settle	babble, buckle, chuckle, demand, direction, fly, helicopter, junction, relate, session, traction	attention, behave, crumble, decide, precise, recess, scribble, sniffle, stubble, trickle	action, blurry, crawl, drifted, helps, horn, hurt, simple, smelling, swelled, torch, yelled	further, hurry, invention, nursery, purple, shelter, smelly, turnips, turtle	depend, gurgle, knuckle, mention, reduction, reorder, throttle, wrinkle	barley, corndog, decoration, drove, nursing, spelling, spurs, sweltering	birdcage, burner, construction, demanding, furnish, hurdle, infection, monkey, northerner, reporting, sawmill, slurp	boiler, cowboy, dirty, foil, joint, jungle, oily, oyster, pointed, soybean, spoiled, twinkle
Sight Words*	brother, mother, other	could, couldn't, should, shouldn't, would, wouldn't	busy	bought, thought	tiny	Review	Review	cried, toward	paper, sorry	beautiful, laugh
Contraction Review					✓ starts					
Reading Long Words	✓	✓	✓	✓		✓	Review	✓	✓	✓
Book Reading	The Train Bob Books C-1	Chickens Bob Books C-1			The Visit Bob Books C-1		Review	Reread favorite stories!	Reread favorite stories!	Reread favorite stories!

*Only newly introduced words listed.

Sound Partners

Lesson Component Scope and Sequence

Scope and Sequence

Sound Partners

LESSONS

COMPONENTS	101	102	103	104	105	106	107	108
New Letter Sounds/Pairs	Review	Review	ow /ō/	Review	ph	Review	Cumulative Review	Cumulative Review
Say the Sounds (and Write Sounds)	broil, destroy, doily, moist, Roy	awnings, decoy, spoiled, tinfoil	blow, borrow, bowl, bowling, bowtie, flow, follow, growing, know, lower, mower, owner, snowball, tow, window, yellow	glowing, slowest, snowstorm, throwing, towboat	alphabet, dolphin, elephant, nephew, phantom, phone, photo, phrase, telegraph	graph, orphan, phase, photo, trophy, typhoon	aw, be-, de-, ey, kn, -le, oi, or, ow, oy, ph, pre-, -tion, ur, wr	er, ey, -le, kn, oi, or, ow, oy, ph, pre-, re-, -sion, -tion, ur, wr
Word Reading (and Spelling)*	employ, enjoy, jiggle, saddle	corduroy, corner, embroider, employment, keychain, loyal, prevention, royalty, Thursday, yawning	lawnmower, owner, prediction, pursue, sorted, towboat, wiggles, willow	bundle, clawing, informed, inspection, joyful, snowplow, sprinkle, stripe	avenue, clues, handle, Memphis, noodle, overdue, partners, phew, Phil, stowaway, telephone, thousands, Troy	enjoyment, marching, moody, photograph, railroad, starving, Tuesday	bottle, elbow, expression, reflection, spine	blade, knight, ointment, rattle, remark, snuggle
Sight Words*	neighbor, through	cookies, eight	enough, lion	cherry, eggs	piece, strange	cold, hold	Review	Review
Reading Long Words	✓	✓	✓	✓	✓	✓	✓	✓
Book Reading	*Poppleton and Friends* Chapter 1 Scholastic Books	*Poppleton and Friends* Chapter 2 Scholastic Books	*Poppleton and Friends* Chapter 3 Scholastic Books	Reread favorite stories!	Reread favorite stories!	Reread favorite stories!	Reread favorite stories!	Reread favorite stories!

*Only newly introduced words listed.

Additional Supplementary Reading
Scope and Sequence

SERIES TITLE	LESSONS									
	21	22	23	24	25	26	27	28	29	30
Primary Phonics		The Cab				The Jet		Gum on a Cat Kim and Wag Mac and Tab The Tin Man Tim Cop Cat Ben Bug Ed Meg Ted The Wig		
Phonics Funnies Storybooks										Not Now
Metropolitan Teaching and Learning Leveled Books Fiction Series									A Bug in the Bathtub	

Additional Supplementary Reading Scope and Sequence

SERIES TITLE	LESSONS									
	31	32	33	34	35	36	37	38	39	40
Primary Phonics				Hal and Nip / The Van and the Hot Rod / Fun in the Mud / The Wet Pup / The Cod and the Fat Cat / Del						
Phonics Funnies Storybooks					A Pet Hen			Grill on the Hill		
Metropolitan Teaching and Learning Leveled Books Fiction Series					A Very Bad Day / What Can Sam Do?				What Was That? / The Sidewalk Toy Stand	

Additional Supplementary Reading Scope and Sequence

Sound Partners

SERIES TITLE	LESSONS									
	41	42	43	44	45	46	47	48	49	50
Primary Phonics									Mole / A Ride on the Bus / The Lie / Babe, the Big Hit / The Bee	
Phonics Funnies Storybooks			Smashed Trash		What a Mess		The Seed	A Little Help / Pack of Snacks / What a Lunch / What Clucks?	A Mouse in the House	The Trip
Metropolitan Teaching and Learning Leveled Books Fiction Series						Do You Like Me? / Have You Met My Pet? / Get Rid of That Dog				Three Pigs and a Wolf

Additional Supplementary Reading Scope and Sequence

SERIES TITLE	51	52	53	54	55	56	57	58	59	60
Primary Phonics		Mac Gets Well The Big Game The Joke The Cake					The Brave Hunter Make the Bed			
Phonics Funnies Storybooks		A New Stew I Want What He Has			Fish Farm		Too Many Ants!	Downtown Clowns		Wall Ball
Metropolitan Teaching and Learning Leveled Books Fiction Series						Can We Have Some? A Hug and Hot Chocolate			Down Mop, Down!	

LESSONS

Additional Supplementary Reading Scope and Sequence

Sound Partners

SERIES TITLE	61	62	63	64	65	66	67	68	69	70
Primary Phonics				A Cow in Town		The Goat		A Fire Coat / Cop Cat and the Mule / Sail / Slide / The Plane Trip		The Seal / Hide and Seek / The Fire / Spot / The Prints
Phonics Funnies Storybooks		A Gray Day / The Boy Who Called Wolf		The Loose Goose / A Hot Book		Where Is the Goat? / All Soaked		Painting a Plain Room / The Rain Stopped		Time to Eat / Three Goats
Metropolitan Teaching and Learning Leveled Books Fiction Series		Make My Day / Our Day With Mom		Is Boo With You? / Did You See Boo? / I Don't Want to Scare You / At the Zoo				The Sitter		Make the Best of It

LESSONS

Additional Supplementary Reading
Scope and Sequence

SERIES TITLE	71	72	73	74	75	76	77	78	79	80
Primary Phonics		A Real Pal Rose and Weed The Deer Ring the Bell	The Dream The Best Gift Mittens The Sea Gull The Square Egg			The Lost Duck Max and the Fox The Chicken Ranch				The Little Skunk The White Hen
Phonics Funnies Storybooks				Some Birthday				The Pot The Sky Is Falling		A Spring Fling Fun in the Sun
Metropolitan Teaching and Learning Leveled Books Fiction Series			No! Not Again!							Better Than You Think The Dog Ate My Homework Pad

Additional Supplementary Reading
Scope and Sequence

Sound Partners

SERIES TITLE	LESSONS									
	81	82	83	84	85	86	87	88	89	90
Primary Phonics							The White Hen The Go-Cart The Lost Horse The Bird Feeder The Hard Worker The Good Cook		The Mouse House The Lost Wallet	
Phonics Funnies Storybooks		A Place by the Lake The Race		A Huge Dog! What's for Dinner?		Good Morning A Bike Ride Fast or First		A Fawn at Dawn	Five or Six	The Man
Metropolitan Teaching and Learning Leveled Books Fiction Series				The Best Pizza Place Good Times at the Lake One Little Tooth			Just a Little Lost and Found		All About Dinosaurs	

Sound Partners

Additional Supplementary Reading
Scope and Sequence

SERIES TITLE	LESSONS									
	91	92	93	94	95	96	97	98	99	100
Primary Phonics				The Pet Poodle A Real Pal					The Shy Tiger	
Phonics Funnies Storybooks		Three Bears			That Hurts			Three Wishes		Too Much Noise
Metropolitan Teaching and Learning Leveled Books Fiction Series		When Will the Sun Come Out? Sidewalk Fun			A Bag for Dad Game Day		Side by Side A Surprise Birthday		Get Down from That Vine!	

Additional Supplementary Reading
Scope and Sequence

Sound Partners

SERIES TITLE	LESSONS							
	101	102	103	104	105	106	107	108
Primary Phonics					Snow Fun Too Small The Clumsy Rabbit			
Phonics Funnies Storybooks			Playing in the Snow The Mouse and the Lion Grow, Little Seed				Too Much Gold	
Metropolitan Teaching and Learning Leveled Books Fiction Series	Rows and Rows of Marigolds This Place Could Shine		You Can Do a Lot with a Lot A Tadpole at the Lake The Pet Show Glide Frog, Glide!			Slide and Ride A Pet for Jed We're Good at Chores		Marta Stays Over

Sound Partners

Appendix

Sound Partners Progress Reports

Single Letters

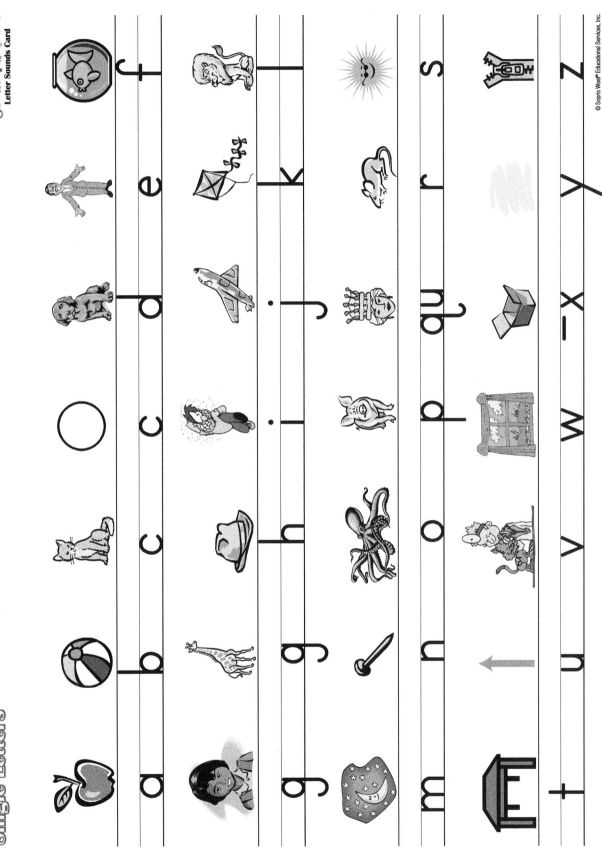

a	b	c	d	e	f
g	g	h	i	j	k	l
m	n	o	p	qu	r	s
t	u	v	w	x	y	z

Sound Partners
Letter Sounds Card

Single Vowels

a e i o u

short vowels

a e o u -y -y

open-syllable vowels

a i o u

magic -e-

© Sopris West® Educational Services, Inc.

Sound Partners

62 Tutor Handbook

© Sopris West® Educational Services, Inc., which grants purchaser permission to photocopy.

Vowel Pairs

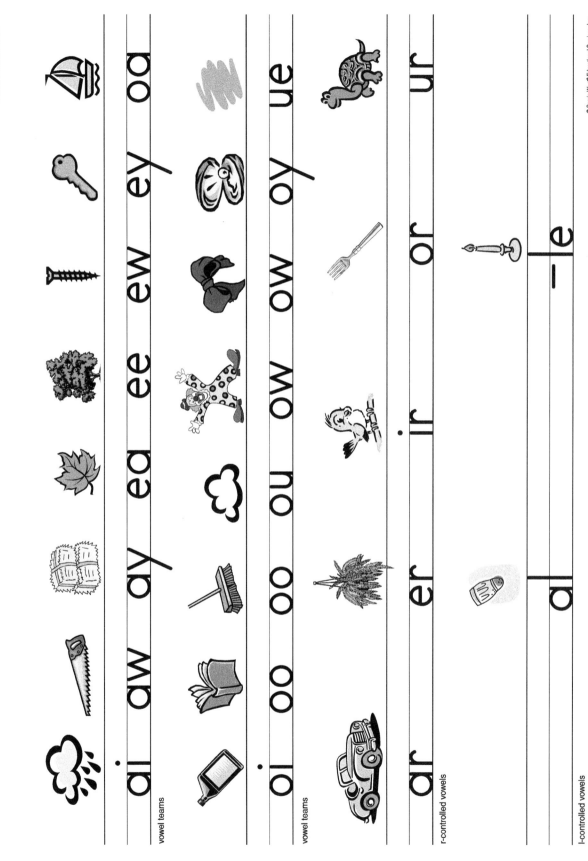

vowel teams — ai aw ay ea ee ew ey oa

vowel teams — oi oo oo ou ow oy ue

r-controlled vowels — ar er ir or ur

l-controlled vowels — al —le

Consonant Digraphs, Blends, and Silent Combinations

ch   —ck   ph   sh   —ng   th   th   wh

consonant digraphs

bl   br   cl   cr   dr   fl   fr   gl   gr   —nk   pl   pr

consonant blends

qu   sc   sk   sl   sm   sn   sp   st   sw   tr   tw

consonant
blends

kn—   wr—

silent consonants

Attendance/Lesson Completion Form

Student: _____ Tutor: _____ School: _____ Month/Year: _____

	MONDAY	TUESDAY	WEDNESDAY	THURSDAY	FRIDAY
	Date: _____	Date: _____	Date: _____	Date: _____	Date: _____
	Tutored? (circle) yes no	Tutored? (circle) yes no	Tutored? (circle) yes no	Tutored? (circle) yes no	Tutored? (circle) yes no
	Lesson(s) #: ☐	**Lesson(s) #:** ☐	**Lesson(s) #:** ☐	**Lesson(s) #:** ☐	**Lesson(s) #:** ☐
	Books Read: _____	**Books Read:** _____	**Books Read:** _____	**Books Read:** _____	**Books Read:** _____
	Date: _____	Date: _____	Date: _____	Date: _____	Date: _____
	Tutored? (circle) yes no	Tutored? (circle) yes no	Tutored? (circle) yes no	Tutored? (circle) yes no	Tutored? (circle) yes no
	Lesson(s) #: ☐	**Lesson(s) #:** ☐	**Lesson(s) #:** ☐	**Lesson(s) #:** ☐	**Lesson(s) #:** ☐
	Books Read: _____	**Books Read:** _____	**Books Read:** _____	**Books Read:** _____	**Books Read:** _____
	Date: _____	Date: _____	Date: _____	Date: _____	Date: _____
	Tutored? (circle) yes no	Tutored? (circle) yes no	Tutored? (circle) yes no	Tutored? (circle) yes no	Tutored? (circle) yes no
	Lesson(s) #: ☐	**Lesson(s) #:** ☐	**Lesson(s) #:** ☐	**Lesson(s) #:** ☐	**Lesson(s) #:** ☐
	Books Read: _____	**Books Read:** _____	**Books Read:** _____	**Books Read:** _____	**Books Read:** _____

Attendance/Lesson Completion Form

Student: _____ Tutor: _____ School: _____ Month/Year: _____

MONDAY	TUESDAY	WEDNESDAY	THURSDAY	FRIDAY
Date: _____ Tutored? (circle) yes no ☐ **Lesson(s) #:** _____ **Books Read:** _____ _____	Date: _____ Tutored? (circle) yes no ☐ **Lesson(s) #:** _____ **Books Read:** _____ _____	Date: _____ Tutored? (circle) yes no ☐ **Lesson(s) #:** _____ **Books Read:** _____ _____	Date: _____ Tutored? (circle) yes no ☐ **Lesson(s) #:** _____ **Books Read:** _____ _____	Date: _____ Tutored? (circle) yes no ☐ **Lesson(s) #:** _____ **Books Read:** _____ _____
Date: _____ Tutored? (circle) yes no ☐ **Lesson(s) #:** _____ **Books Read:** _____ _____	Date: _____ Tutored? (circle) yes no ☐ **Lesson(s) #:** _____ **Books Read:** _____ _____	Date: _____ Tutored? (circle) yes no ☐ **Lesson(s) #:** _____ **Books Read:** _____ _____	Date: _____ Tutored? (circle) yes no ☐ **Lesson(s) #:** _____ **Books Read:** _____ _____	Date: _____ Tutored? (circle) yes no ☐ **Lesson(s) #:** _____ **Books Read:** _____ _____

Notes: _____
_____
_____

Tutor Observation Form

Tutor: _____   Date: _____

Observer: _____   Student: _____

Lesson: _____   School: _____

Directions:
If the observer arrives late (does not observe the criterion) or if the criterion is not applicable at the time, leave blank.

Instructional Component	Criteria	Never	Rarely	Sometimes	Mostly	Always
Say the Sounds	Adheres to lesson directions/script. ____ Models new sounds in boxes. ____ Models correct/clear sounds. ____ Checks that student produces sounds correctly. ____ Has student write three sounds.	1	2	3	4	5
	Notes:					
Segmenting	Adheres to lesson directions/script. ____ Models activity, as scripted as listening task. ____ Has student point to boxes when segmenting.	1	2	3	4	5
	Notes:					
Word Reading	Adheres to lesson directions/script. ____ Models words in boxes. ____ Requires student to attempt/demonstrate sounding out words correctly. ____ Provides listening practice on new/difficult sounds.	1	2	3	4	5
	Notes:					
All Spelling Tasks	Adheres to lesson directions/script. ____ Chooses three spelling words that match student needs. ____ Has student read all written words.	1	2	3	4	5
	Notes:					
Sight Words	Adheres to lesson directions/script. ____ Models new words in boxes. ____ Requires student to read, point, and orally spell word. ____ Reviews weak/new sight words where directed.	1	2	3	4	5
	Notes:					
All Sentence, Text, and Book Reading Tasks	Adheres to lesson directions/script. ____ Spends 10–15 minutes on book reading. ____ Requires student to fingerpoint. ____ Requires student to reread fluently if error made. ____ Tutor rereads sentence when needed to refresh meaning. ____ Reads new book twice, then reads previous books. ____ Reads repeated book once, then reads previous books.	1	2	3	4	5
	Notes:					

Tutor Observation Form

Tutor: _____ Date: _____

Observer: _____ Student: _____

Lesson: _____ School: _____

Instructional Component	Criteria	Never	Rarely	Sometimes	Mostly	Always
Magic-e-	Adheres to lesson directions/script. _____ Follows script changes as scaffolding reduces. _____ Corrects by reminding student of rule/noticing word ending.	1	2	3	4	5
	Notes:					
Word Endings	Adheres to lesson directions/script. _____ Models by pointing and saying word with ending. _____ Says words aloud for student to repeat with ending. _____ Has student read words.	1	2	3	4	5
	Notes:					
Letter Card Use	Adheres to lesson directions/script. _____ Chooses the best task for student, based on skill. _____ Follows directions for the task.	1	2	3	4	5
	Notes:					

Tutor Behavior	Criteria	Never	Rarely	Sometimes	Mostly	Always
Instructional Delivery	Maximizes time on instruction.	1	2	3	4	5
	Quick pace/smooth transitions/minimal pauses.	1	2	3	4	5
	Uses appropriate specific praise.	1	2	3	4	5
	Provides appropriate error correction/scaffolding.	1	2	3	4	5
	Materials are organized.	1	2	3	4	5
	Maintains accurate attendance records.	1	2	3	4	5

Feedback to Tutor

Mastery Test Directions for Administration and Scoring

Administer each Mastery Test soon after the student has completed every tenth lesson. Use the Mastery Test to check that the student has learned the skills taught in those lessons and to gauge how much review to provide. The Mastery Tests are best administered by someone other than the student's regular tutor, although we know this can be difficult to arrange.

The Mastery Tests can also be used by the program supervisor to place a student who needs to start further along in the lessons. Find the Mastery Test on which the student scores less than 90% (e.g., Mastery Test 4, Lessons 31–40) and begin instruction at that point in the lessons (i.e., start at Lesson 31).

Materials

- ▶ Tester copy of Mastery Test
- ▶ Student copy of Mastery Test
- ▶ Student Recording Sheet
- ▶ Pencils for student and tester

Administration

1. Place student copy of Mastery Test in front of student.

2. Place your copy of Mastery Test in a position so that the student cannot see what you read or record.

3. Say the directions provided for each part of the test on the tester copy. There are three test parts: Sounds (saying the sounds and writing the sounds), Word Reading/Sight Word Reading, and Spelling.

4. Mark incorrect student responses with a slash.

5. Add the total correct responses for each part. (Add the responses for both saying sounds and writing sounds for the Sounds total.)

6. For Sounds writing and Spelling words, have the student use the Student Recording Sheet.

7. At the end of testing, review the student's scores. For any section on which the test indicates more review, incorporate this review into your regular instruction.

Scoring

1. If the student cannot identify a letter sound or read a word within three seconds, score the item incorrect and move to the next item. Say, "Let's try the next one."

2. If the student makes an error and then corrects the error within three seconds, score the item as correct.

3. Remind the student to write clearly so that you can distinguish correct spelling.

4. Do not penalize the student for imprecise pronunciation due to dialect, articulation, or second-language issues. Use your knowledge of how the student usually pronounces sounds to decide whether the student is producing his or her closest approximation to the correct sound.

Suggestions

1. If you (the tutor) are using the Mastery Test to monitor student progress, and your student scores below 70%, talk to your supervisor. Review whether you are implementing the lessons correctly, and have your supervisor observe and provide suggestions.

2. Keep a file of each student's Mastery Tests so that you can refer to these tests to monitor student progress over time. Share the tests with the classroom teacher for use in instructional decision-making.

Mastery Test 1—Tester Recording Sheet

Tutor: _____

Student: _____

Date: _____

School: _____

Sounds

▶ "Point to each letter. Say the sound."

Put a slash through incorrect responses.

h	m	a
s	t	n
d	o	c

Number Correct
_____ / 9

▶ *Dictate sounds for student to write.*

🖊 "Write the letter that makes the _____ sound."

/a/	/s/	/n/
/c/	/h/	/d/
/m/	/t/	/o/

▶ *Use key words from Letter Sounds Cards (e.g., /a/ as in <u>apple</u>).*

Put a slash through incorrect responses.

(Provide student with **Mastery Test 1—Student Recording Sheet**, which follows this test.)

a	s	n
c	h	d
m	t	o

Number Correct
_____ / 9

TOTAL for Sounds	_____ / 18

17 / 18 = 94%	16 / 18 = 89% 15 / 18 = 83%	14 / 18 = 78% or less
Go forward.	*Review missed items, then move forward.*	*Review this set of letter sounds.*

Tutor: _____   Date: _____

Student: _____   School: _____

mad	hot	cod
dot	cat	sad
and	ham	had
sat	Sam	Mac

Word Reading

▶ "Sound these words out, then read them fast."

Put a slash through incorrect responses.

TOTAL for Word Reading	_____ / 12	
11 / 12 = 92%	10 / 12 = 83%	9 / 12 = 75% or less
Go forward.	Review missed items, then move forward.	Review this set of lessons; give more practice reading words with missed letter sounds.

(Provide student with **Mastery Test 1—Student Recording Sheet**, which follows this test.)

dot	mat
man	tot
Sam	and
cot	not
hat	mad

Spelling

"I say the word, and you write the word."

▶ *Have student write these words on the Student Recording Sheet.*

Put a slash through incorrect responses.

TOTAL for Spelling	_____ / 10	
9 / 10 = 90%	8 / 10 = 80%	7 / 10 = 70% or less
Go forward.	Review missed items, then move forward.	Review this set of lessons; give more practice spelling words with missed letter sounds.

Sound Partners

Mastery Test 1—Student Recording Sheet

Tutor: _____   Date: _____

Student: _____   School: _____

Sounds (Writing)

Spelling

Mastery Test 2—Tester Recording Sheet

Tutor: _____   Date: _____

Student: _____   School: _____

LESSONS 11–20

Sounds

▶ "Point to each letter. Say the sound."

Put a slash through incorrect responses.

g   r   b

i   p   w

j   o   d

Number Correct
_____ / 9

▶ *Dictate sounds for student to write.*

(Provide student with **Mastery Test 2—Student Recording Sheet**, which follows this test.)

"Write the letter that makes the _____ sound."

/g/	/r/	/b/
/i/	/p/	/w/
/j/	/o/	/d/

g   *r*   *b*

i   *p*   *w*

j   *o*   *d*

▶ *Use key words from Letter Sounds Cards (e.g., /a/ as in apple).*

Put a slash through incorrect responses.

Number Correct
_____ / 9

TOTAL for Sounds	_____ / 18
17 / 18 = 94%	16 / 18 = 89% 15 / 18 = 83%	14 / 18 = 78% or less
Go forward.	*Review missed items, then move forward.*	*Review this set of letter sounds.*

Mastery Test 2—Tester Recording Sheet

Tutor: _____ Date: _____

Student: _____ School: _____

jog	rat	big
tin	wag	hop
mop	dim	pad
win	hit	jam

Word Reading

▶ "Sound out these words, then read them fast."

Put a slash through incorrect responses.

TOTAL for Word Reading	_____ / 12	
11 / 12 = 92%	10 / 12 = 83%	9 / 12 = 75% or less
Go forward.	*Review missed items, then move forward.*	*Review this set of lessons; give more practice reading words with missed letter sounds.*

(Provide student with **Mastery Test 2—Student Recording Sheet**, which follows this test.)

pit	dip
got	jam
rid	wig
pan	bad
wag	ran
job	bog

Spelling

✎ "I say the word, and you write the word."

▶ *Have student write these words on the Student Recording Sheet.*

Put a slash through incorrect responses.

TOTAL for Spelling	_____ / 12	
11 / 12 = 92%	10 / 12 = 83%	9 / 12 = 75% or less
Go forward.	*Review missed items, then move forward.*	*Review this set of lessons; give more practice spelling words with missed letter sounds.*

Tutor: _____   Date: _____

Student: _____   School: _____

Sight Word Reading

▶ "Read these words."

Put a slash through incorrect responses.

you	is	the	of
his	to	has	as

TOTAL for Sight Word Reading	_____ / 8
7 / 8 = 88%	6 / 8 = 75% or less
Review missed items, then move forward.	*Review this set of sight words; give more practice reading and spelling words.*

Mastery Test 2—Student Recording Sheet

Tutor: _____   Date: _____

Student: _____   School: _____

Sounds (Writing)

Spelling

Mastery Test 3—Tester Recording Sheet

Tutor: _____   Date: _____

Student: _____   School: _____

LESSONS 21–30

Sounds

▶ "Point to each letter or letter pair. Say the sound."

Put a slash through incorrect responses.

u	f	e
th	k	l
x	i	b

Number Correct
_____ / 9

▶ *Dictate sounds for student to write.*

✏ "Write the letter(s) that makes the _____ sound."

/u/	/f/	/e/
/th/	/k/	/l/
/x/	/i/	/b/

▶ *Use key words from Letter Sounds Cards (e.g., /a/ as in <u>apple</u>).*

Put a slash through incorrect responses.

Number Correct
_____ / 9

(Provide student with **Mastery Test 3—Student Recording Sheet,** which follows this test.)

u	f	e
th	k	l
x	i	b

TOTAL for Sounds	_____ / 18

17 / 18 = 94%	16 / 18 = 89% 15 / 18 = 83%	14 / 18 = 78% or less
Go forward.	*Review missed items, then move forward.*	*Review this set of letter sounds.*

Tutor: _____   Date: _____

Student: _____   School: _____

bud   fix   fed

let   bath   wet

path   red   box

kid   log   fun

Word Reading

▶ "Sound out these words, then read them fast."

Put a slash through incorrect responses.

TOTAL for Word Reading	_____ / 12	
11 / 12 = 92%	10 / 12 = 83%	9 / 12 = 75% or less
Go forward.	*Review missed items, then move forward.*	*Review this set of lessons; give more practice reading words with missed letter sounds.*

(Provide student with **Mastery Test 3—Student Recording Sheet**, which follows this test.)

bug   hug
fed   fan
path   wet
keg   that
lid   kid
fox   lot

Spelling

"I say the word, and you write the word."

▶ *Have student write these words on the Student Recording Sheet.*

Put a slash through incorrect responses.

TOTAL for Spelling	_____ / 12	
11 / 12 = 92%	10 / 12 = 83%	9 / 12 = 75% or less
Go forward.	*Review missed items, then move forward.*	*Review this set of lessons; give more practice spelling words with missed letter sounds.*

Tutor: _____   Date: _____

Student: _____   School: _____

**Sight Word
Reading**

said	for	can't	were
come	he	some	we

▶ "Read these
words."

*Put a slash through
incorrect responses.*

TOTAL for Sight Word Reading	_____ / 8
7 / 8 = 88%	**6 / 8 = 75% or less**
Review missed items, *then move forward.*	*Review this set of sight words;* *give more practice reading and spelling words.*

Mastery Test 3—Student Recording Sheet

Tutor: _____   Date: _____

Student: _____   School: _____

Sounds (Writing)

Spelling

Mastery Test 4—Tester Recording Sheet

Tutor: _____   Date: _____

Student: _____   School: _____

LESSONS 31–40

Sounds

▶ "Point to each letter or letter pair and say the sound."

Put a slash through incorrect responses.

Number Correct
_____ / 9

v   y   z

sh   ch   wh

e   th   u

▶ Dictate sounds for student to write.

✏ "Write the letter(s) that makes the _____ sound."

/v/	/y/	/z/
/sh/	/ch/	/wh/
/e/	/th/	/u/

▶ Use key words from Letter Sounds Cards (e.g., /a/ as in <u>apple</u>).

Put a slash through incorrect responses.

Number Correct
_____ / 9

(Provide student with **Mastery Test 4—Student Recording Sheet**, which follows this test.)

v   y   z

sh   ch   wh

e   th   u

TOTAL for Sounds	_____ / 18	
17 / 18 = 94%	16 / 18 = 89% 15 / 18 = 83%	14 / 18 = 78% or less
Go forward.	*Review missed items, then move forward.*	*Review this set of letter sounds.*

Sound Partners

Mastery Test 4—Tester Recording Sheet

Tutor: _____   Date: _____

Student: _____   School: _____

Word Reading

▶ "Sound out these words, then read them fast."

Put a slash through incorrect responses.

fix	vex	yap
chop	yes	bash
zip	dish	whip
vet	rich	yet
such	wham	shop

TOTAL for Word Reading	_____ / 15

14 / 15 = 93%	13 / 15 = 87%	12 / 15 = 80% or less
Go forward.	Review missed items, then move forward.	Review this set of lessons; give more practice reading words with missed letter sounds.

(Provide student with **Mastery Test 4—Student Recording Sheet**, which follows this test.)

Spelling

"I say the word, and you write the word."

▶ *Have student write these words on the Student Recording Sheet.*

Put a slash through incorrect responses.

van	chin
yap	shed
fix	much
zip	when
bash	yes
whip	vet

TOTAL for Spelling	_____ / 12

11 / 12 = 92%	10 / 12 = 83%	9 / 12 = 75% or less
Go forward.	Review missed items, then move forward.	Review this set of lessons; give more practice spelling words with missed letter sounds.

Mastery Test 4—Tester Recording Sheet

Tutor: _____   Date: _____

Student: _____   School: _____

LESSONS 31–40

they	I'll	what	saw
there	was	I'm	all
you'll	I	what's	

Sight Word Reading

▶ "Read these words."

Put a slash through incorrect responses.

TOTAL for Sight Word Reading	_____ / 11

10 / 11 = 91%	9 / 11 = 82%	8 / 11 = 73% or less
Go forward.	*Review missed items, then move forward.*	*Review this set of sight words; give more practice reading and spelling words.*

Mastery Test 4—Student Recording Sheet

Tutor: _____   Date: _____

Student: _____   School: _____

Sounds (Writing)

Spelling

Tutor: _____ Date: _____

Student: _____ School: _____

Sounds

▶ "Point to each letter or letter pair. Say the sound."

Put a slash through incorrect responses.

Number Correct
_____ / 12

qu	fl	sk
sl	er	ee
st	ck	ou
tr	ue	sw

▶ *Dictate sounds for student to write.*

"Write the letters that make the _____ sound."

/qu/	/fl/	/sk/
/sl/	/er/	/sw/
/ee/	/st/	/ck/
/ou/	/tr/	/ue/

▶ *Use key words from Letter Sounds Cards (e.g., /a/ as in <u>apple</u>).*

Put a slash through incorrect responses.

Number Correct
_____ / 12

(Provide student with **Mastery Test 5—Student Recording Sheet**, which follows this test.)

qu	fl	sk
sl	er	sw
ee	st	ck
ou	tr	ue

TOTAL for Sounds	_____ / 24

23 / 24 = 96% 22 / 24 = 92%	21 / 24 = 88% 20 / 24 = 83%	19 / 24 = 79% or less
Go forward.	*Review missed items, then move forward.*	*Review this set of letter sounds.*

Tutor: _____   Date: _____

Student: _____   School: _____

LESSONS 41–50

quilt	skid	sheet
hunter	swims	whiz
flash	skip	fern
need	slash	luck
couch	outer	glue

Word Reading

▶ "Sound out these words, then read them fast."

Put a slash through incorrect responses.

| TOTAL for Word Reading | _____ / 15 |

14 / 15 = 93%	13 / 15 = 87%	12 / 15 = 80% or less
Go forward.	Review missed items, then move forward.	Review this set of lessons; give more practice reading words with missed letter sounds.

(Provide student with **Mastery Test 5—Student Recording Sheet**, which follows this test.)

quiz	blue
flash	cloud
feel	true
stack	duck
sweeps	hunter
queen	trout

Spelling

"I say the word, and you write the word."

▶ *Have student write these words on the Student Recording Sheet.*

Put a slash through incorrect responses.

| TOTAL for Spelling | _____ / 12 |

11 / 12 = 92%	10 / 12 = 83%	9 / 12 = 75% or less
Go forward.	Review missed items, then move forward.	Review this set of lessons; give more practice spelling words with missed letter sounds.

Mastery Test 5—Tester Recording Sheet

Tutor: _____   Date: _____

Student: _____   School: _____

LESSONS 41–50

Sight Word Reading

▶ "Read these words."

Put a slash through incorrect responses.

over	mouse	she	by
she's	my	house	want

TOTAL for Sight Word Reading	_____ / 8
7 / 8 = 88%	6 / 8 = 75% or less
Review missed items, then move forward.	*Review this set of sight words; give more practice reading and spelling words.*

Mastery Test 5—Student Recording Sheet

Tutor: _____ Date: _____

Student: _____ School: _____

Sounds (Writing)

Spelling

Sound Partners

Mastery Test 6—Tester Recording Sheet

Page 1 of 3

Tutor: _____   Date: _____

Student: _____   School: _____

LESSONS
51–60

Sounds

▶ "Point to each letter or letter pair. Say the sound."

Put a slash through incorrect responses.

Number Correct
_____ / 12

ew	-y	ar
ow	al	gr
ou	ue	ee
er	qu	tr

- -

▶ *Dictate sounds for student to write.*

✏ "Write the letter(s) that make the _____ sound."

/ew/	/-y/	/ar/
/ow/	/al/	/gr/
/ou/	/ue/	/ee/
/er/	/qu/	/tr/

▶ *Use key words from Letter Sounds Cards (e.g., /a/ as in <u>apple</u>).*

Put a slash through incorrect responses.

(Provide student with **Mastery Test 6—Student Recording Sheet**, which follows this test.)

ew	-y	ar
ow	al	gr
ou	ue	ee
er	qu	tr

Number Correct
_____ / 12

- -

TOTAL for Sounds	_____ / 24

23 / 24 = 96% 22 / 24 = 92%	21 / 24 = 88% 20 / 24 = 83%	19 / 24 = 79% or less
Go forward.	Review missed items, then move forward.	Review this set of letter sounds.

© Sopris West® Educational Services, Inc., which grants purchaser permission to photocopy.

Tutor: _____   Date: _____

Student: _____   School: _____

LESSONS 51–60

Word Reading

▶ "Sound out these words, then read them fast."

Put a slash through incorrect responses.

artist	wheeled	cry
hard	marker	stewing
brow	shy	shower
calm	salty	farmer
now	chart	bright

TOTAL for Word Reading	_____ / 15

14 / 15 = 93%	13 / 15 = 87%	12 / 15 = 80% or less
Go forward.	*Review missed items, then move forward.*	*Review this set of lessons; give more practice reading words with missed letter sounds.*

(Provide student with **Mastery Test 6—Student Recording Sheet**, which follows this test.)

Spelling

🖉 "I say the word, and you write the word."

▶ *Have student write these words on the Student Recording Sheet.*

Put a slash through incorrect responses.

trouser	quart
weeds	power
drew	starting
yarn	stall
ball	chew
bark	sly

TOTAL for Spelling	_____ / 12

11 / 12 = 92%	10 / 12 = 83%	9 / 12 = 75% or less
Go forward.	*Review missed items, then move forward.*	*Review this set of lessons; give more practice spelling words with missed letter sounds.*

Tutor: _____   Date: _____

Student: _____   School: _____

any	head	knew	have
live	very	says	know
one	many	two	house

Sight Word Reading

▶ "Read these words."

Put a slash through incorrect responses.

TOTAL for Sight Word Reading	_____ / 12	
11 / 12 = 92%	10 / 12 = 83%	9 / 12 = 75% or less
Go forward.	*Review missed items, then move forward.*	*Review this set of sight words; give more practice reading and spelling words.*

Mastery Test 6—Student Recording Sheet

Tutor: _____   Date: _____

Student: _____   School: _____

Sounds (Writing)

Spelling

Mastery Test 7—Tester Recording Sheet

Tutor: _____   Date: _____

Student: _____   School: _____

LESSONS 61–70

ay	oo	oa
oo	ai	ea
al	ow	ew
ue	ou	er

Sounds

▶ "Point to each letter pair. Say the sound."

Put a slash through incorrect responses.

Number Correct
_____ / 12

(Provide student with **Mastery Test 7—Student Recording Sheet**, which follows this test.)

ay	oo	oa
oo	ai	ea
al	ow	ew
ue	ou	er

▶ Dictate sounds for student to write.

✏ "Write the letters that make the _____ sound."

/ay/	/oo/	/oa/
/oo/	/ai/	/ea/
/al/	/ow/	/ew/
/ue/	/ou/	/er/

▶ Use key words from Letter Sounds Cards (e.g., /a/ as in <u>apple</u>).

Put a slash through incorrect responses.

Number Correct
_____ / 12

TOTAL for Sounds	_____ / 24	
23 / 24 = 96% 22 / 24 = 92%	21 / 24 = 88% 20 / 24 = 83%	19 / 24 = 79% or less
Go forward.	Review missed items, then move forward.	Review this set of letter sounds.

Sound Partners

Tutor: _____   Date: _____

Student: _____   School: _____

Word Reading

▶ "Sound out these words, then read them fast."

Put a slash through incorrect responses.

playing	book	loafing
room	stray	roasted
sailing	tooth	dealer
brain	failed	cartoons
treats	layer	float

TOTAL for Word Reading	_____ / 15
14 / 15 = 93%	13 / 15 = 87%	12 / 15 = 80% or less
Go forward.	Review missed items, then move forward.	Review this set of lessons; give more practice reading words with missed letter sounds.

(Provide student with **Mastery Test 7—Student Recording Sheet**, which follows this test.)

Spelling

"I say the word, and you write the word."

▶ *Have student write these words on the Student Recording Sheet.*

Put a slash through incorrect responses.

payday	boots
crook	floated
toast	sailing
paid	strainer
treat	meanest
mighty	taller

TOTAL for Spelling	_____ / 12
11 / 12 = 92%	10 / 12 = 83%	9 / 12 = 75% or less
Go forward.	Review missed items, then move forward.	Review this set of lessons; give more practice spelling words with missed letter sounds.

Tutor: _____   Date: _____

Student: _____   School: _____

don't	their	find	we've
who	eyes	from	are
no	kind	aren't	so
go	we'll		

Sight Word Reading

▶ "Read these words."

Put a slash through incorrect responses.

TOTAL for Sight Word Reading	_____ / 14	
13 / 14 = 93%	12 / 14 = 86%	11 / 14 = 79% or less
Go forward.	*Review missed items, then move forward.*	*Review this set of sight words; give more practice reading and spelling words.*

Mastery Test 7—Student Recording Sheet

Tutor: _____   Date: _____

Student: _____   School: _____

Sounds (Writing)

Spelling

Sound Partners

Mastery Test 8—Tester Recording Sheet

Tutor: _____   Date: _____

Student: _____   School: _____

LESSONS 71–80

ir   kn   wr

–ng   –nk

Sounds

▶ "Point to each letter pair. Say the sound."

Put a slash through incorrect responses.

Number Correct
_____ / 5

(Provide student with **Mastery Test 8—Student Recording Sheet,** which follows this test.)

ir   *kn*   *wr*

–ng   *–nk*

▶ *Dictate sounds for student to write.*

✎ "Write the letters that make the _____ sound."

/ir/   /kn/   /wr/
/-ng/   /-nk/

▶ *Use key words from Letter Sounds Cards (e.g., /a/ as in* apple*).*

Put a slash through incorrect responses.

Number Correct
_____ / 5

TOTAL for Sounds	_____ / 10

9 / 10 = 90%	8 / 10 = 80%	7 / 10 = 70% or less
Go forward.	*Review missed items, then move forward.*	*Review this set of letter sounds.*

Tutor: _____   Date: _____

Student: _____   School: _____

birthday	knee	hanging
stringy	finger	honk
knight	tanker	slingshot
yanked	knife	wrench
wreath	thirsty	junk

Word Reading

▶ "Sound out these words, then read them fast."

Put a slash through incorrect responses.

TOTAL for Word Reading	_____ / 15

14 / 15 = 93%	13 / 15 = 87%	12 / 15 = 80% or less
Go forward.	*Review missed items, then move forward.*	*Review this set of lessons; give more practice reading words with missed letter sounds.*

(Provide student with **Mastery Test 8—Student Recording Sheet**, which follows this test.)

tanker	girls
strong	kneecap
clanging	lungs
wrench	blink
knob	wrist
shirt	knit

Spelling

"I say the word, and you write the word."

▶ *Have student write these words on the Student Recording Sheet.*

Put a slash through incorrect responses.

TOTAL for Spelling	_____ / 12

11 / 12 = 92%	10 / 12 = 83%	9 / 12 = 75% or less
Go forward.	*Review missed items, then move forward.*	*Review this set of lessons; give more practice spelling words with missed letter sounds.*

Tutor: _____   Date: _____

Student: _____   School: _____

Sight Word Reading

▶ "Read these words."

Put a slash through incorrect responses.

| your | where | talk | because |
| walk | put | four | both |

TOTAL for Sight Word Reading	_____ / 8
7 / 8 = 88%	6 / 8 = 75% or less
Review missed items, then move forward.	*Review this set of sight words; give more practice reading and spelling words.*

Mastery Test 8—Student Recording Sheet

Tutor: _____   Date: _____

Student: _____   School: _____

Sounds (Writing)

Spelling

Mastery Test 9—Tester Recording Sheet

Page 1 of 3

Tutor: _____   Date: _____

Student: _____   School: _____

LESSONS
81–90

Sounds

▶ "Point to each letter or letter pair. Say the sound."

▶ "Say the **soft** sounds for the <u>c</u> and <u>g</u>."

Put a slash through incorrect responses.

Number Correct
_____ / 6

c   g   or

aw   er   ir

- -

▶ *Dictate sounds for student to write.*

✏ "Write the letter(s) that makes the _____ sound."

/c/   /g/   /or/
/aw/   /er/   /ir/

▶ *Use key words from Letter Sounds Cards (e.g., /a/ as in <u>apple</u>).*

Put a slash through incorrect responses.

(Provide student with **Mastery Test 9—Student Recording Sheet**, which follows this test.)

c   g   or

aw   er   ir

Number Correct
_____ / 6

- -

TOTAL for Sounds	_____ / 12

11 / 12 = 92%	10 / 12 = 83%	9 / 12 = 75% or less
Go forward.	*Review missed items, then move forward.*	*Review this set of letter sounds.*

© Sopris West® Educational Services, Inc., which grants purchaser permission to photocopy.

Tutor: _____   Date: _____

Student: _____   School: _____

cinder	germ	forbid
morning	crawling	age
face	pencil	sorting
straw	energy	hawk
paws	circus	cent

Word Reading

▶ "Sound out these words, then read them fast."

Put a slash through incorrect responses.

TOTAL for Word Reading	_____ / 15

14 / 15 = 93%	13 / 15 = 87%	12 / 15 = 80% or less
Go forward.	*Review missed items, then move forward.*	*Review this set of lessons; give more practice reading words with missed letter sounds.*

(Provide student with **Mastery Test 9—Student Recording Sheet**, which follows this test.)

acid	page
outlaw	ginger
cigar	border
corner	straw
center	place
shortest	ice

Spelling

"I say the word, and you write the word."

▶ *Have student write these words on the Student Recording Sheet.*

Put a slash through incorrect responses.

TOTAL for Spelling	_____ / 12

11 / 12 = 92%	10 / 12 = 83%	9 / 12 = 75% or less
Go forward.	*Review missed items, then move forward.*	*Review this set of lessons; give more practice spelling words with missed letter sounds.*

Tutor: _____   Date: _____

Student: _____   School: _____

do   move   friend   sure

little   shiny   again

Sight Word Reading

▶ "Read these words."

Put a slash through incorrect responses.

TOTAL for Sight Word Reading	_____ / 7
6 / 7 = 86%	5 / 7 = 71% or less
Review missed items, then move forward.	*Review this set of sight words; give more practice reading and spelling words.*

Mastery Test 9—Student Recording Sheet

Tutor: _____   Date: _____

Student: _____   School: _____

Sounds (Writing)

Spelling

Tutor: _____   Date: _____

Student: _____   School: _____

LESSONS 91–108

Sounds

▶ "Point to each letter pair or word part. Say the sound."

Put a slash through incorrect responses.

–le	be–	de–
pre–	re–	ir
–tion	–sion	ur
ey	oi	oy
ow	ph	

Number Correct
_____ / 14

(Provide student with **Mastery Test 10—Student Recording Sheet**, which follows this test.)

▶ *Dictate sounds for student to write.*

"Write the letters that make the _____ sound."

–le	be–	de–
pre–	re–	–tion
–sion	ur	ey
oi	oy	ow
ph		

/-le/	/be-/	/de-/
/pre-/	/re-/	/-tion/
/-sion/	/ur/	/ey/
/oi/	/oy/	/ow/
/ph/		

▶ *Use key words from Letter Sounds Cards (e.g., /a/ as in apple).*

Put a slash through incorrect responses.

Number Correct
_____ / 13

TOTAL for Sounds	_____ / 27

26 / 27 = 96% 25 / 27 = 93%	24 / 27 = 89% 23 / 27 = 85% 22 / 27 = 82%	21 / 27 = 78% or less
Go forward.	*Review missed items, then move forward.*	*Review this set of letter sounds.*

Mastery Test 10—Tester Recording Sheet

Page 2 of 3

Tutor: _____ Date: _____

Student: _____ School: _____

Word Reading

▶ "Sound out these words, then read them fast."

Put a slash through incorrect responses.

blow	alphabet	owner
loyal	spoiled	turkey
dribble	mission	action
prevent	repay	burst
began	detach	tickle
remote	beside	delight

TOTAL for Word Reading	_____ / 18

17 / 18 = 94%	16 / 18 = 89% 15 / 18 = 83%	14 / 18 = 78% or less
Go forward.	Review missed items, then move forward.	Review this set of lessons; give more practice reading words with missed letter sounds.

(Provide student with **Mastery Test 10—Student Recording Sheet**, which follows this test.)

pointed	friction
hockey	belong
hurt	prevent
buckle	simple
mission	defend

Spelling

"I say the word, and you write the word."

▶ *Have student write these words on the Student Recording Sheet.*

Put a slash through incorrect responses.

TOTAL for Spelling	_____ / 10

9 / 10 = 90%	8 / 10 = 80%	7 / 10 = 70% or less
Go forward.	Review missed items, then move forward.	Review this set of lessons; give more practice spelling words with specific word parts.

Tutor: _____   Date: _____

Student: _____   School: _____

Sight Word Reading

▶ "Read these words."

Put a slash through incorrect responses.

brother	should	busy	bought
sorry	beautiful	laugh	thought
wouldn't	mother	could	hold
piece	strange	cold	other
neighbor	through	eight	cookies
enough	lion	cherry	eggs
paper	toward	cried	tiny

TOTAL for Sight Word Reading	_____ / 28	
26 / 28 = 95% 25 / 28 = 90%	24 / 28 = 86%	23 / 28 = 81% or less
Go forward.	Review missed items, then move forward.	Review this set of sight words; give more practice reading and spelling words.

Mastery Test 10—Student Recording Sheet

Tutor: _____   Date: _____

Student: _____   School: _____

Sounds (Writing)

<table>
<tr><td></td><td></td><td></td></tr>
<tr><td></td><td></td><td></td></tr>
<tr><td></td><td></td><td></td></tr>
<tr><td></td><td></td><td></td></tr>
<tr><td></td><td></td><td></td></tr>
</table>

Spelling

<table>
<tr><td></td><td></td></tr>
<tr><td></td><td></td></tr>
<tr><td></td><td></td></tr>
<tr><td></td><td></td></tr>
<tr><td></td><td></td></tr>
</table>

Sound Partners Progress Report 1

Tutor: _____   Date: _____

Student: _____   School: _____

Dear Teacher: These are the skills I have most recently worked on with my *Sound Partners* tutor.

			New Letter Sounds
a	m	s	
t	c	d	
n	o	h	

				Words
am	Dan	on	Sam	
hot	mad	cot	dot	
nod	sat	and	had	
at	not	ham	Tom	
cat	hat	dad	mom	

Tutor Notes and Observations:

Sound Partners Progress Report 2

Tutor: _____   Date: _____

Student: _____   School: _____

Dear Teacher: These are the skills I have most recently worked on with my *Sound Partners* tutor.

g		r		b
i		p		w
j		o		d

New Letter Sounds

got	ran	mop	jig
wig	rag	sob	jam
in	job	dog	dim
bog	rig	big	wit
rid	nap	rip	bin

Words

you	is	the	of
his	to	has	as	isn't

Sight Words

Tutor Notes and Observations:

Sound Partners **Progress Report 3**

Tutor: _____ Date: _____

Student: _____ School: _____

Dear Teacher: These are the skills I have most recently worked on with my *Sound Partners* tutor.

u		f		e
th	k		l	x

New Letter Sounds

up	lot	fox	cup
mix	fans	bud	jut
bath	fun	that	thin
fig	pen	lids	fed
Kip	mill	let	fog

Words

can't	didn't	come	some	be
he	me	we	said	it's
let's	for	or	into	were

Sight Words

Tutor Notes and Observations:

Sound Partners Progress Report 4

Tutor: _____   Date: _____

Student: _____   School: _____

Dear Teacher: These are the skills I have most recently worked on with my *Sound Partners* tutor.

				New Letter Sounds
v	y		z	
sh	ch		wh	

				Words
flip	when	sand	whip	
yak	vet	such	chin	
rich	zap	shut	yet	
fizz	sham	crash	fish	
chug	fix	chop	yes	

				Sight Words
was	they	I	all	
what	I'm	I'll	you'll	
saw	there	what's		

Tutor Notes and Observations:

Sound Partners Progress Report 5

Tutor: _____ Date: _____

Student: _____ School: _____

Dear Teacher: These are the skills I have most recently worked on with my *Sound Partners* tutor.

qu	fl	sk	sl	er	ee	**New Letter Sounds**
st	sw	ck	ou	tr	ue	

crunched	slouch	mouth	quack	**Words**
rusty	canteen	coffee	skated	
ouch	fast	crew	fern	
true	under	faster	quiz	
steep	cheeks	bumper	swims	

over	she	she's	want	**Sight Words**
my	by	house	mouse	

Tutor Notes and Observations:

Sound Partners Progress Report 6

Tutor: _____   Date: _____

Student: _____   School: _____

Dear Teacher: These are the skills I have most recently worked on with my *Sound Partners* tutor.

New Letter Sounds

final y (as in fly)   ar (as in car)   al (as in salt)

ew (as in screw)   ow (as in clown)   gr (as in grape)

Words

newer	shy	sky	harp
supply	parking	hard	flew
yarn	darker	salty	start
stewing	brow	outing	taller
farmer	shower	quacks	scald

Sight Words

any	many	head	knew	know
have	two	says	very	one	live

Tutor Notes and Observations:

Sound Partners **Progress Report 7**

Tutor: _____   Date: _____

Student: _____   School: _____

Dear Teacher: These are the skills I have most recently worked on with my *Sound Partners* tutor.

New Letter Sounds

ay (as in hay)   oo (as in moon)   oo (as in book)

oa (as in boat)   ai (as in rain)   ea (as in leaf)

Words

clay	coat	payday	tools
playing	book	loaf	room
stray	roasted	sailing	tooth
dealer	brain	failed	cartoons
treats	layer	float	wheat

Sight Words

don't	who	from	their	are
aren't	no	go	so	we've
we'll	kind	find	eyes	

Tutor Notes and Observations:

Sound Partners Progress Report 8

Tutor: _____   Date: _____

Student: _____   School: _____

Dear Teacher: These are the skills I have most recently worked on with my *Sound Partners* tutor.

New Letter Sounds

ir (as in bird)   kn (as in knot)   wr (as in wreck)

−ng (as in long)   −nk (as in drink)

Words

birch	wrong	clanging	first
knee	birthday	hanging	honk
yanked	knife	wrench	wreath
thirsty	junk	string	unwrap
stinking	wrapper	knead	

Sight Words

both	where	walk	talk
because	put	your	four

Tutor Notes and Observations:

Sound Partners **Progress Report 9**

Tutor: _____   Date: _____

Student: _____   School: _____

Dear Teacher: These are the skills I have most recently worked on with my *Sound Partners* tutor.

New Letter Sounds

soft c (as in circle)   soft g (as in giraffe)   or (as in fork)

aw (as in saw)

Words

cinder	germ	forbid	morning
crawling	age	face	pencil
ginger	popcorn	circus	sorting
seesaw	center	ordering	dawn
straw	cent	outlaw	glory

Sight Words

do	move	friend	sure
little	shiny	again	

Tutor Notes and Observations:

Tutor: _____   Date: _____

Student: _____   School: _____

Dear Teacher: These are the skills I have most recently worked on with my *Sound Partners* tutor.

New Letter Sounds

ur (as in turtle)   oi (as in oil)   ph (as in phone)

ey (as in key)   oy (as in oyster)   ow (as in bow)

−tion (as in action)   −sion (as in vision)   be− (as in beside)

de− (as in delight)   re− (as in reheat)   pre− (as in preschool)

−le (as in candle)

Words

purple	showtime	towboat	nursing
honey	money	broiler	spoiled
alphabet	owner	loyal	turkey
dribble	mission	action	prevent
repay	began	detach	tickle
remote	beside	delight	predict

Tutor Notes and Observations:

Sound Partners

Tutor: _____   Date: _____

Student: _____   School: _____

Dear Teacher: These are the skills I have most recently worked on with my *Sound Partners* tutor.

Sight Words

busy	thought	bought	tiny
toward	sorry	paper	laugh
beautiful	through	neighbor	cookies
eight	enough	lion	eggs
cherry	strange	piece	hold
cold	other	mother	brother
cried	could	would	should
couldn't	wouldn't	shouldn't	

Tutor Notes and Observations: